THE CHRISTIAN WAY
—REALITY OR ILLUSION?

The Christian Way
—Reality or Illusion?

Alexander J. M. Wedderburn

CASCADE *Books* • Eugene, Oregon

THE CHRISTIAN WAY—REALITY OR ILLUSION?

Copyright © 2015 Alexander J. M. Wedderburn. All rights reserved. Except for brief quotations in critical publications or reviews, no part of this book may be reproduced in any manner without prior written permission from the publisher. Write: Permissions, Wipf and Stock Publishers, 199 W. 8th Ave., Suite 3, Eugene, OR 97401.

Cascade Books
An Imprint of Wipf and Stock Publishers
199 W. 8th Ave., Suite 3
Eugene, OR 97401

www.wipfandstock.com

ISBN 13: 978-1-4982-0249-7

Cataloging-in-Publication data:

Wedderburn, A. J. M.

    The Christian way—reality or illusion? / Alexander J. M. Wedderburn.

    viii + 80 p.; 23 cm—Includes bibliographical references.

    ISBN 13: 978-1-4982-0249-7

    1. Jesus Christ. 2. Liberalism (Religion). 3. Christian ethics. I. Title.

BR1615 W435 2015

Manufactured in the USA.

©New Revised Standard Version Bible, copyright 1989, Division of Christian Education of the National Council of the Churches of Christ in the United States of America. Used by permission. All rights reserved.

Table of Contents

Preface vii
1. In Quest of "Reality" 1
2. Celebrating the Birth of Jesus 11
3. Following Jesus 28
4. Remembering the Death of Jesus 54
5. Living the Resurrection of Jesus? 64
6. Epilogue 74
For Further Reading 79

Preface

Like my previous work *The God of Jesus—Our God?* this little book is written under circumstances that prevent me from having access to libraries, except electronically, and from coping with printed matter in any quantity. The result is again a book that makes little reference to secondary literature and avoids any amassing of detail, but that may as a result be rather easier to read. Or so I hope.

In a sense, too, this study takes up from where that earlier work left off. For that left open the question how far Jesus' God could ever be ours. If one could no longer invoke any supernatural or other-worldly power as Jesus did or if any power that there may be is so ill-defined and mysterious that it offers little practical orientation, does that mean that the entire Christian movement is based on an illusion, namely that the way followed by Christians is guided by some such power and has in that its *raison d'être*? Or does the Christian tradition offer a different basis that does not presuppose the other-worldly, but is rooted in the this-worldly and still makes sense and is of value? Tentatively this little study dares to answer "Yes."

Again I am very much indebted to Cascade Books and Wipf & Stock Publishers and their staff for undertaking to publish this work, but especially to Dr. Robin Parry who has edited it. I am very grateful, too, for the support

PREFACE

and encouragement of a number of friends and colleagues (although probably very few of them will agree with my conclusions), but above all, once again, to my wife Brigitte.

1

In Quest of "Reality"

"Reality" is a somewhat elusive term. For a start, that elusiveness is not helped by the way in which "real" and "unreal" are used in more or less clearly subjective senses. The statement that "the experience was very real to me" more or less gives itself away by the superlative. On the other hand, there are experiences that may seem "unreal," but are in fact real, as in the case of many natural wonders: a sunset may seem as if it could have been painted by someone, or the plumage of a bird may be so exotic, as in the case of a bird of paradise, that one could think that some human hand had stuck those splendid feathers on. "Very real" experiences of the sort alluded to above make us ready to make confident assertions about them, and what we have experienced is then, for us, "real, reality." And often we may be right to claim that, but at other times we may be mistaken, not about our feeling of certainty or conviction that something is the case, but mistaken about the *truth* of what we assert to be true. The truth may then dawn ("I could have sworn that X," "I was sure that Y," or the like), but sometimes it may not.

Again, modern media have clouded the issue with talk of "reality television" and "virtual reality." The former actually often or usually involves situations that are unreal in the sense of being artificial or contrived, recalling animals on display in a zoo or performing in a circus, except that the participants are conscious human beings who are allowing themselves to be put in the situation in question (and being paid for it). The "reality" involved is thus in some considerable measure unreal. The latter expression covers thoroughly pragmatic and beneficial uses of media technology in training programs such as flight simulation for pilots, but also the use of the expression for such technologies employed in the service of computer games and the like, where the "reality" involved may *seem* very "real," but where the experience involved is of more questionable benefit. This is particularly the case when the distinction between the virtual and the real is blurred or when the virtual even becomes more real than the real world for the person concerned.

Yet there is, too, a sense in which we subjectively have confidence that we are in fact dealing with what is real, and correspondingly the language of "reality" may be used in a more objective sense, particularly of things in the present, and especially when our experience of these things is shared and corroborated by others. Of things in the past, on the other hand, it is better to speak of what is more or less probable or, at best, beyond all reasonable doubt. In the present, however, some things seem to be certainties—that it is daytime (at least where we are located on the globe), that it is cloudy or rainy (unless we happen to be in the make-believe world of a cinema set), that we live in a town or the country (unless we find ourselves on the outermost edge of an urban sprawl in which the distinction can get blurred). Such things are, at any rate, pretty tangible or recognizable

IN QUEST OF "REALITY"

by the senses and are inter-personal in the sense that we find others who share them and confirm them.

It is true that there are problems in linking "reality" with the experiences of our senses. In the history of philosophy there are those who have preferred the trustworthiness of the immediate experiences of our senses and have reduced reality to a world of "sense-data." Today the opposite is more often the case in that physicists have taught us to regard seemingly solid objects as in fact made up of myriads of forces and particles that are not detectable to the senses left to their own resources. Nonetheless, that has not prevented most of us from treating the objects that we see and touch as in varying degrees solid, so that we are often prepared to commit our weight and our lives to them. We are, in short, prepared to treat them as part of the "real world" in which we live.

It is, however, altogether another matter when we come to talk of what is sometimes referred to as "the world of the spirit" or of "spiritual things," and at first sight that is the case when we come to speak of the Christian church and the Christian faith. Nonetheless, it is an undeniable reality that there exists in the world a great number of persons and groups that claim to belong to the Christian church. Their existence and presence seems tangible enough, whether they mark their presence with imposing or not-so-imposing buildings or advertise themselves and their existence less obviously. Sometimes they will make their claim to do so in an inclusive way, not wishing to deny the claims of other persons and groups also to belong to this church. Others will be more exclusive in their claim, maintaining that either they alone or perhaps also a few others from this great mass of claimants really belong to the church. And for the most part even those broadest in their tolerance of the claims of others will probably place a question-mark against a number of groups, often labeling them as "sects," perhaps particularly in the case of some groups that most hotly claim that they are the true followers of God and Jesus. Or there are some groups, such as the Quakers, that are no longer agreed amongst themselves whether they belong to the Christian church or not (there are often evidently enough who say that they do for them to be represented in some way or other in Christian ecumenical institutions and councils).

The existence of this institution, the Christian church, and these groups that go to make it up, is a reality, a sociological entity whose existence few would question, however much they may argue about what makes it or them tick and even more about its or their right to exist. And it is here that a far more difficult and contentious question about reality emerges: does this entity point to a reality lying beyond itself, so that its existence is the product of, and a testimony to, that reality? In other words, whereas one can in one sense speak of the Christian church as undeniably a reality, there is the further question whether, if the deeper reality to which it claims to point should be, in fact, illusory, the historical and social reality of the Christian church is a deception. For it founds its existence on certain claims, not just on the sheer fact that it exists. But, if these claims should prove unfounded, does that mean that its members are mistaken or deluded? And that is a question that can be posed, not just in relation to the institution as a whole, but also with regard to a whole series of rites and beliefs that give the Christian church its shape and form and the Christian faith its content. So, for some critics, Christianity seems to belong to the world of make-believe, a set of stories permeated with magical acts and strange powers like so many fairy-stories. It might be likened to a tantalizingly deceptive mirage in the midst of the spiritual desert that is our world.

Now I have chosen to pose the question "reality or illusion?" in terms of the "Christian way," the life of faith lived in many different ways by members of the Christian church. With regard to this way it is appropriate and in keeping with this image of a way to ask about its goal and whether that goal is real or illusory. That is naturally a question that arises for many in relation to an afterlife, a life beyond this world and the grave, but it is also a question posed when one speaks of God or the heavenly Christ as that goal. Yet the afterlife, God, and Christ as a heavenly person are all alike shrouded in mystery, and the reality of the Christian way seems to elude us if we attempt a definition of the goal of the Christian way in these terms alone. Or can the way and its goal, which provides the travellers on it with their orientation, be defined in ways that are more tangible and not so inscrutable? I avoid introducing such terms as Bonhoeffer's "religionless Christianity" or the now more common "secular Christianity" here, in part because of the suspicion that the use of such labels may hinder the careful analysis of exactly what is being said on each occasion, in part because the latter term in particular seems to cover a wide field of views. For a start, if Christianity lets itself be guided and shaped by Jesus and his teaching, albeit critically evaluated, then this is not the same as appealing to generally recognized norms and criteria (if there are such and if that is what "secular" could be supposed to mean), even if the source of this guidance is this-worldly.

Naturally this question of the truth of Christianity and the reality that it represents is not new; it has existed from the very beginnings of Christian faith. It was answered in various ways, but above all by appeal to the person of Jesus of Nazareth, whom his followers gave the title "Christ," that is "the anointed one (of God)," so much so that it became for them and much of the world around them a proper name peculiar to him. The claims that they made for Jesus were couched in the terminology and the thought-world of their day, and therein lies a problem for another age such as ours to which much of this terminology and this thought-world are alien and hard to understand, let alone endorse. It is true that there are a great many Christians for whom the language and the ideas of those bygone ages are sacrosanct and must be preserved unquestioned and unchallenged, valid today as much as they were then. Yet it is clear from the New Testament and even more so from the early Christian apologists from the second century onwards that the Christian claims for Jesus were bolstered by drawing on the ideas of contemporary philosophical thought and made use of the motifs and images of the myths of the time, both to illustrate the significance of Jesus and also to show how he surpassed these non-Christian parallels. Above all appeal was made to the writings of the Jewish Scriptures and other early Jewish texts to show Jesus as the fulfillment of the expectations that early Christians found there or read into these texts. Such an appeal was often achieved at the cost of offering some readings of those texts that were at variance with their likely original meaning and also at the cost of importing improbable elements into the story of Jesus' life. (A much quoted example is Matthew 21:5–7, where Zechariah 9:9's reference to Jerusalem's king coming to it seated on an ass and on a colt the foal of an ass is interpreted so that Jesus seems to ride *both beasts simultaneously*, whereas the prophet's words refer but to one animal, the second being but a more exact description of the first. Mark and Luke sensibly mention only the colt, sparing us the impression that Jesus may have been engaged in some circus act.) Among some conservative Christians today such literal readings of the Scriptures are still in vogue, combined with the conviction that, as the very word or words of Israel's and the Christians' God, they must be true, perhaps with the occasional concession to the possible use of figurative language (e.g., the "days" of creation as in fact longer periods of time, on the grounds that a thousand years are but as a day in God's sight—Psalm 90:4).

I must confess that originally, in my student days, I espoused one version of such a Christian fundamentalist position, often with an obnoxious zeal and bigotry such that I blush at the memory of the excesses to which such a position inevitably led. My intellectual history since then has been one of a gradual sloughing off and discarding of many of these beliefs and views, coming to see them as unnecessary, time-conditioned, often even morally or theologically objectionable today; nor are they warranted by the Christian foundational documents, above all those of the Christian New Testament, once those writings are approached as what they are, historical and time-conditioned documents, and are critically examined as such. In other words, I have come to regard the view that we have divinely inspired and infallible words in these writings as a delusion, together with much that might flow from that premise, such as a literal interpretation of the account of creation. And much the same is true of the often widely differing ways and practices of the various Christian traditions that have evolved over the centuries, so that these traditions often seem to function as a straitjacket constricting the expression of Christian faith today. That is true even of the way that I view the figure of Jesus of Nazareth and the layers of Christian dogma that have surrounded his person, along with the often highly elaborate views of God's person, which I now regard as thoroughly speculative. That these speculations correspond to the reality of a divine being I am also inclined to regard as illusory.

Yet stripping off what I regard as unnecessary accretions does leave me with the question, "What is then left of the Christian faith?" It is true that the reality of the Christian church, with its great variety of forms and beliefs, some of them irreconcilable with one another, remains, but is this entity by itself anything more than an empty shell? Is it not rather like a couple of teams of football players set on a playing field without a ball? They might be choreographed to go through the motions of playing (perhaps with the occasional foul to add to the interest and realism), but the point of the whole exercise would be lacking. It would be hard to be satisfied with the notion of the Christian church in all its forms acting similarly and simply going through the motions of being a worshipping community, without reference to any reality beyond itself and its own existence. That would seem to be a rather drastic case of make-believe. So what reality, if any, could stand beyond these various manifestations of the life of the Christian community?

As a consequence of raising this question I have chosen to look at various central aspects of Christian experience and practice, grouping them together under the term "the Christian way," and asking what remains when we take into account the elements that have been added on to the foundational events of this faith. Some elements must, I believe, be discarded as untrue or unhelpful, others may deserve the status of stories and legends that have a symbolic value, illuminating in an appropriate way the reality to which they bear witness.

And yet the choice of the term "the Christian way" might seem to demand some justification, in that it places the emphasis above all on ethics, on a way of life practiced and preached by the Christian church and to some extent stemming from Jesus himself, and that is something on which the third chapter of this little work will concentrate. For some, this concentration may seem natural if they are among those who have narrowed down the relevance of the message of Jesus to a matter of ethics, for example, to a matter of the love of one's neighbor and the ability to accept oneself. And for many non-Christians it is this, and this alone, which they regard as valuable about Christianity as a whole. (Gandhi springs to mind as an example here, but there are many, especially in an increasingly secular Western world, that consider themselves as in some way Christian in this sense, but not as members of the Christian church.) It is true that such an admiration of the ethical teaching of Jesus may involve a certain degree of selectivity, for there are surely aspects of Jesus' ethical teaching, such as the sanctions and penalties with which he threatens those who do not heed his message, that are not usually regarded as part of the ethic that such people admire. It is true that some of the less attractive features of Jesus' teaching may have been put on his lips later by his followers. Some of the sharp polemic against the Jewish teachers and religious leaders of his time may, for instance, bear the mark of the conflicts that later arose between the early church and their fellow Jews, as portrayed in the early chapters of the Acts of the Apostles. The command to love one's enemies seems here to have been hard to apply. This enmity seems to be reflected in the way that the Fourth Gospel denounces "the Jews" (e.g., John 8:44) or where Paul or a Christian tradition speaks of God's wrath having overtaken the Jewish people at last (1 Thess 2:14–16); it no longer seems to be a matter of denunciation of the religious leaders of Israel as in Matthew 23, but to be far more general and sweeping in its condemnation. And down the centuries even relations between Christian and Christian have often been far from manifesting anything that we would today want to describe as love, except in the most perverted sense; it is scarcely surprising, then, that Jews, Muslims, and those of other beliefs have also suffered much at the hands of Christians. This is all, sadly, part of the reality that Christianity has been, a reality that, we may rightly conclude, contradicts the very roots and basis of this faith. In the light of this long and sad tale of an anything but loving Christianity is it not imperative that it is the ethical demands of the Christian message that should be given the highest priority?

For those, on the other hand, who belong to the Christian church and take part in its life there are many aspects of their life and practice that do not simply come under the heading of ethics, and may indeed figure more prominently and assume a greater importance in their experience as Christians than the demands of ethical teaching. These aspects (such as worship, rites, festivals) are part of the reality of the Christian church as they experience it. Yet the question remains how far such this-worldly, human reality—for it is in itself no more than something this-worldly—in fact points to some greater reality, and how these aspects serve their purpose in living the Christian life. Often the appeal is made back to the past, the time of Jesus and the early church, and the beliefs that were held then, but often these ancient beliefs can be regarded as false or at best questionable. Yet can such aspects then just be discarded without loss of meaning or worth, just as some have discarded God from the Christian worldview? And do the various rites and the like—that for many are an integral part of the Christian life and way—in fact serve a useful purpose in living that life or do they rather distort, or distract from, that way?

2

Celebrating the Birth of Jesus

"Celebration" is an apt word to use in the case of the birth of Jesus when one considers how much has been built up around this event. By that I mean not just the paraphernalia and accessories associated with the season of Advent and Christmas, which make their presence felt in shops and elsewhere on the coat-tails of summer, if not earlier. For a massive theological weight has also traditionally been loaded upon this event, as the "incarnation," the becoming flesh of the very person of God, so that the child that is born is none other than God walking in the midst of our world.

What has been built up around this event is impressive enough and at the same time distracts us quite tragically from the event itself, particularly if we concentrate upon that event stripped of its later theological trappings. Much was appended to the New Testament accounts already in early Christian tradition (e.g., names for the three star-gazing sages from the east that came to pay homage to Jesus) and those accounts themselves often reflect theological concerns rather than historical memory, and moreover reflect different theological concerns. For even some quite conservative scholars have concluded that the two accounts that we have, in the Gospels of Matthew and Luke, cannot be made to agree with one another. Thus we cannot be sure even whether Jesus was born in Bethlehem rather than in Galilean Nazareth where he later grew up. There is good cause to doubt the story of the census that allegedly brought Joseph and Mary to Bethlehem. Such a census was usual Roman practice when a province was added to the Roman Empire, but would not have occurred while Rome's trusty ally Herod the Great still ruled in Palestine. The mention of the governor of the neighboring province of Syria, Quirinius, makes a date following the deposition by the Romans in the year 6 of the Common Era of one of Herod's sons, Archelaus, more plausible (as Rome took over, under their own direct control, that part of Herod's far more extensive domains that Archelaus ruled). But that cannot be reconciled with a dating of Jesus' birth during Herod the Great's time (i.e., before 4 BCE). Nor is it clear why such a census would require Joseph, let alone Mary, to travel from Nazareth in Galilee, where they resided already according to Luke 1:26, to Bethlehem in Judea. It would, however, be more convenient for Luke's account of Mary visiting her cousin Elizabeth in the Judean hills (1:39) if they had been resident in Bethlehem, for the journey from Nazareth would be a longer one, involving passing through Samaria. Matthew's story, on the other hand, suggests that they originally lived in Bethlehem, fled to Egypt for fear of Herod's fearful elimination of potential rivals, and only returned after that king's death, choosing a new place of residence in the area now ruled by one of his sons. (Archelaus, who now ruled Judea, came to have a bad reputation if he did not already have one.)

Yet Jesus' followers had good cause to want the birth to take place in Bethlehem. For one thing, Nazareth was not highly regarded by some of Jesus' contemporaries, as we see when John's Gospel makes Nathanael ask whether anything good can come from that place (1:46). And, more positively, it was expected that a future ruler of Israel would come from Bethlehem, the home of King David, as prophesied by Micah 5:2. So Matthew 2:6 has Herod the Great consult his experts and then directs the wise men from the east to look there if they want to find the ruler whom the star foretells.

Yet this is apparently no ordinary ruler for Matthew or for Luke, but one born of a virgin through the direct intervention of God, through God's spirit, "the power of the Most High" (Luke 1:35). Admittedly these two Gospels are alone in this, since the Fourth Gospel tells a different story of the incarnation of the divine Word, with no mention of, or presumably need for, a human mother, and, even more strikingly, Mark's Gospel does not mention the circumstances of Jesus' birth at all, nor any of his life up to that point when he comes to John the Baptist to be baptized by him (Mark 1:9). Again, however, in addition to the parallels that can be found in pagan myths of the time, the Jewish Scriptures have probably played their part in the formation of this version of the story of Jesus' birth. For the Greek translation of Isaiah 7:14, quoted in Matthew 1:23, speaks of a *parthenos* conceiving and bearing a son who shall be called Emmanuel, "God with us." English translations will often keep "the virgin" in Matthew, but prudently bear in mind the likely meaning of the Hebrew in translating Isaiah (so, e.g., the New Revised Standard Version, "the young woman," a far less loaded translation).

These two versions of the story of Jesus' birth have obviously had an enormous influence on those branches of the Christian church where Jesus' mother is particularly venerated, but it is the version found in the Fourth Gospel that has played a far greater role in the history of Christian doctrine. For, whereas in Matthew and Luke God's son comes into being through his birth from the womb of a human mother, John's Gospel tells of the entry into the world and into the form of human flesh of a pre-existent being, designated as the Logos or "Word," that had already been with God "in the beginning." However, this way of viewing the person of Jesus had, to put it mildly, problems. For Christian orthodoxy wished to insist on the full humanity of Jesus, although some groups on the fringes of the Christian church solved that problem by denying this reality of Jesus' full humanity, and down the years Christians who wished to espouse the traditional doctrine have yet strayed into utterances and ways of thinking that make it questionable how full his humanity in fact was. (There is a well-known and well-loved Christmas carol, "Away in a manger," that at one point asserts that the child Jesus did not cry. The writer may only have been thinking of a particular moment of peace, yet nonetheless the impression remains that this child was above such things.) If it was difficult to see how one who was at the same time God could be fully human, it was equally difficult to see how a divine being could be human without impairing the possession of those qualities associated with divinity. That problem was all the more acute in that early Christians operated here within the categories, constraints, and presuppositions of the philosophy and theology of the Greco-Roman world around them, and sought their solutions to these problems within that framework. However satisfying these solutions may have seemed then—and what emerged as a majority consensus in the creeds of the church emerged only at the cost of much strife, pain, and vilifying of one's opponents—, the categories of thought and the arguments that were used and found favor then are for most of us not those that we would find useful or convincing today.

CELEBRATING THE BIRTH OF JESUS

John and the Synoptics

The Gospel of John played a dominant role in these arguments, yet it is notoriously difficult to hold together the picture of Jesus yielded by this Gospel with that which we gain from the other three canonical Gospels, the Synoptics. The difference between the birth of Jesus from a human mother sits uneasily alongside the appearance of a pre-existent divine being such as the Prologue of John envisages. And whereas the Jesus of the Synoptics may be limited in his knowledge (Mark 13:32/Matt 24:36), the Johannine Jesus is even aware of the glory that he shared with his Father before the world was made (John 17:5). And in contrast to the agony of doubt and terror with which the Jesus of the first three Gospels approaches his death (Mark 14:36; 15:34/Matt 26:39; 27:46/Luke 22:42), John's Jesus has power to lay down his life and take it up again (John 10:18). It is no wonder that some have called the full humanity of John's Jesus into question. One can see why John has so emphasized Jesus's divine stature as a retort to Jewish critics who questioned and rejected it, but there has been a heavy price to pay for this one-sided emphasis in terms of intelligibility and indeed of a sense of reality.

Matthew and Luke's accounts of Jesus' birth are surrounded with manifestations of the supernatural such as appearances of angels and an archangel and a sign in the stars, yet the fundamental event is very much down to earth, whether that earth be that of Bethlehem or Nazareth. If doubts surround it then those doubts above all concern the paternity of Jesus. These two evangelists wish it to be understood that God is Jesus' father, but evidence of alternative explanations emerge sooner or later in Christian and above all Jewish tradition, such as the suggestion that Mary had been the victim of rape. Less spectacular might be the explanation that Joseph had been a bit premature and had exercised his marital rights while still only engaged rather than properly married—something that would occasion little surprise in some, though not all, Christian circles today, but found less acceptance among pious Jews then. (Mark 6:3 may be significant here, for those who hear Jesus in his home town there refer to him as the carpenter and son of Mary and refer to his brothers and sisters, but not, as would be more customary, to his father. In contrast and, despite the birth narrative of chapters 1 and 2, Matthew 13:55 has them refer to him as the "carpenter's son" and Luke 4:22 refers to him as Joseph's son, with no mention of Mary or siblings, let alone of God.)

Whatever one decides about Jesus' paternity, and whether one locates his birth in his Galilean home or in a stable in Bethlehem, it is clear that this was no unmistakable birth of a princely figure, let alone a divine one. Rightly, Luke 1:47 makes Mary in the hymn that we know as the Magnificat refer to her low social status. That relatively low status is underlined, at least symbolically, if not historically, by Luke's account of the homage offered to the child by shepherds (2:8–18), a social group which also had no high social standing. From all that we know of Jesus' subsequent life this impression of a humble beginning, if not utter poverty, is a reality that should not be allowed to be overshadowed and obscured by such trappings as those with which these two accounts have invested it, be it heavenly visions, meteorological or cosmic signs, or visitations by more distinguished worshippers from the east. The last-named, however, may still retain a certain symbolic significance, bearing witness to the opening up of the reality of what had happened to a wider world. Nonetheless, the reality is that of a defenseless child of lowly status and perhaps also a doubtful paternity, hardly conforming to the usual pattern of a divine manifestation.

This disclosure is celebrated by Christians in the four-week season of Advent ("coming") as well as the following twelve days of Christmas. It is important, however, to focus on what really came then, for this coming tends to be obscured by other "comings." Quite apart from the coming of the episcopal Sankt Niklaus and his entourage on December 6 and the many comings of Father Christmas or Santa Claus (for the bishop tends to get merged with this figure in the popular mind) in all sorts of contexts (e.g., shops and parties) up till the official one on the night of December 24, Christian worship and reflection during this time has tended to echo language from passages in the Jewish Scriptures that speak of the final and glorious coming of the Jewish God. So the German Advent hymn "Macht hoch die Tür" (in English-speaking hymnody found in a form like "Lift up your heads, O ye gates") echoes the triumphant language of Psalm 24:7–10, "Lift up your heads, O gates, . . . that the King of glory may come in; . . . the Lord, strong and mighty, . . . mighty in battle; . . . the Lord of hosts, . . . the King of glory." It is hard to imagine a greater contrast with what was actually to be seen at Jesus' coming, so that one has to ask whether such hymns do not distract from the mystery and the challenge that the reality of the event that took place then presents. For the finality and glory implicit in such allusions distract from the *in*glorious nature of the reality of Jesus' birth, and what followed it was certainly not that final denouement that Jewish psalms and prophets had hailed.

However, even more than the possible distractions presented by the various trappings that the two gospel accounts of his conception and birth in Matthew and Luke present, there is a far greater danger in the story told by the Gospel of John, which says nothing explicitly about

Jesus' conception and birth. Here is one who became flesh (John 1:14) but nevertheless can look back to a glory that he shared with his heavenly Father before the ages (17:5). He is one who dies, as is the lot of all human beings, yet it is a matter of laying down a life which he, unlike all other human beings, has the power and authority to take up again (10:17–18). Essential elements of the usual human experience of life in this world seem to be lacking, so that some have accused this evangelist of presenting us with a Jesus who only *seems* to be human. And that is surely a considerable barrier that prevents us being able to identify ourselves with him and his life.

Moreover, as already mentioned, this sort of understanding of Jesus' nature seems hard to reconcile with the picture of Jesus that we find in the other three canonical Gospels. There, as we saw, Jesus is in ignorance of the timing of the end that he foresees, that being God's privilege alone (Mark 13:32/Matt 24:36). Here the reference to "the Son," which is far more characteristic of the Fourth Gospel, is unusual in the Synoptic Gospels and probably points there to the work of a later hand; nevertheless, the fact that this later hand preserves this limitation of Jesus' knowledge of events distinguishes this utterance from Johannine theology, if not from Johannine terminology. Yet it is above all when we come to Jesus' sufferings and death that we find a markedly different picture. In the first place Jesus, confronted with the fate that he sees before him as he prays in Gethsemane, only reluctantly accepts that this is the way that he must go (Mark 14:36/Matt 26:39). In contrast, in John's equivalent to this prayer, set slightly earlier in his narrative of events (John 12:27), Jesus firmly sets aside the possibility that he should be saved from this hour, for it is for this purpose that he has come to this hour. And it is in Matthew and Mark's account of the crucifixion that Jesus cries out reproachfully, asking why his God has deserted him (Mark 15:34/Matt 27:46). John's Jesus, on the other hand, breathes his last with a triumphant cry to the effect that it, his work, is completed (19:30).

A Human Figure?

The picture that follows the birth or, in Mark's case, the baptism of Jesus in the first three canonical Gospels is in keeping with the all too human death of Jesus at the end. The child that is born grows up to manhood but is seemingly unaware of anything that would make him superhuman. It is true that he makes considerable claims for himself, claims to authority and to act in God's name, performing wonders of healing and of other sorts. He sees God's finger at work in his driving out of demons (Luke 11:20; Matt 12:28 has "spirit" instead of "finger"). Yet in most of this activity he stands in the tradition of Jewish prophets before him and seems to be aware of the prophetic role that he fulfills (e.g., Luke 13:33). That is scarcely surprising in one who let himself be baptized by the prophet John and then carried on a preaching ministry that shared many of the traits of John's message, nor is it surprising that many of his contemporaries saw him in the same light. It is true that he may have spoken of something greater being experienced in his ministry than in that of Jonah (Matt 12:41/Luke 11:32), but it is to be noted that he does not say "some*one* greater." There is no hint that he in his humanity was any in this respect any different to Jonah and the other prophets.

In all this he was not alone among his contemporaries, for he involved an inner circle of disciples in his work, giving them too the authority to preach, to heal, and to cast out demons. For we have in the gospel traditions accounts of Jesus commissioning disciples, either twelve or seventy(-two) to carry on his work, making it known and available to a wider circle (cf. Mark 6:7–13; Luke 10:1–12). Even when Jesus gives one of the clearest signs of his conviction that God was at work in his ministry in the driving out of demons mentioned in Luke 11:20; Matt 12:28, it is in the context of the work of his disciples that Jesus saw the downfall of Satan (Luke 10:18). (That holds good if in fact the context in which Luke places the saying is the original one; for if on the contrary it was uttered by Jesus either with regard to some visionary experience of his own, e.g., at his baptism, or in connection with one of his own exorcisms, then this tells us nothing about his evaluation of the exorcisms performed by his followers. Nonetheless, it would then be striking that Luke has chosen to put it in this context.) The reality of this ministry and this work was thus a shared one, and it would be rash to question the reality of all of this. It is true that some of the wonders attributed to Jesus may reflect the expectations of the time or reflection upon Old Testament precedents, but others may be explicable in terms of the potentialities of the human psyche. At any rate there are similar claims made for Christian charismatic circles today, however one may evaluate them. If there are many who would claim to have been healed in some way or other in such Christian groups, there is little reason to doubt that there were those in first-century Palestine who believed the same to be true in their own experience, whether it was Jesus or one of dis disciples who had acted in God's name to heal them.

It may be, too, that the question of his relationship to the Jewish expectation of God's "anointed one," the Messiah, coming in the end time, may have crossed Jesus' mind, just as it probably occurred to some of his contemporaries. Yet whatever answer he or they gave to this question it is to be noted that, like the prophets, the Messiah was a *human* figure. Whether he appeared on earth or in the clouds of heaven he does not seem to have been regarded as divine, and indeed that sort of claim might have conflicted with Jewish monotheistic beliefs. Just as important at this point is the observation that Jesus was not one to limit to his own person this authority or this work that he believed God had given him. There is a strand in the Jesus-tradition of what has been called a "democratization" of messianic ideas and figures in the Old Testament (so Gerd Theissen and Christopher Tuckett), a "collective" understanding of that role. By that it is meant that Jesus took up themes and tasks that in Jewish expectations were variously attributed to an individual figure, the Messiah, and invited and called his immediate followers to share those tasks with him. Besides the commissioning of disciples to carry out his work that we have already noted, in the future, too, the smaller group of twelve disciples was evidently destined for the kingly role of judgment, sitting on thrones to judge Israel (Matt 19:28/ Luke 22:30). In Luke 12:32 Jesus again seems to promise his disciples kingly rule—God would give them kingly rule. Luke 22:29 ("And I confer a kingdom on you just as my Father has conferred a kingdom on me") would be even clearer, although one might question how far Jesus actually would have felt that he had the authority to confer such a kingdom. Yet, even if this is a later formulation, the idea of the kingly rule of the disciples is clear. For, when a kingdom is given to someone, that person functions as a ruler. That can be seen in Daniel 7:27, "The kingdom and dominion and the greatness of the kingdoms under the whole heaven shall be given to the people of the holy ones of the Most High; their kingdom shall be an everlasting kingdom, and all dominions shall serve and obey them" (New Revised Standard Version). Does that apply as well to the promise given to the poor in the beatitude of Luke 6:20 where the kingdom is promised to them? While we may more often think of this as allowing them to enter into God's kingdom or to share in the good things that the kingdom brings, the doxology of the Lord's Prayer that has later been added to that prayer uses a similar phrase, "Thine is the kingdom" (Matthew 6:13, according to some witnesses); that hardly refers to God's entry into the kingdom or sharing in its good things, but rather to God's kingly rule. What is then to prevent us interpreting the promise to the poor as also meaning that they will share in exercising God's kingly rule—a reversal of their present position of weakness? This promise also seems to apply to children, according to Mark 10:14 (cf. Matthew 19:14; Luke 18:16): "Allow the children to come to me and do not prevent them; for to such as these God's kingdom belongs." And such a ruling in the eschatological kingdom of God would in those days without doubt be seen as a function of the Messiah.

In all these texts, it is striking that they do not exalt Jesus to a position above the whole of the rest of humanity, let alone above human existence itself, and that is a strong argument for the trustworthiness of this tradition. To this line of argument should be added the common fate and lot that Jesus shared with his disciples: they share his homelessness (Luke 9:58/Matt 8:20) and his renunciation of life in his family, and must reckon with sharing his suffering by bearing their own cross (Luke 14:27/Matt 10:38; cf. Mark 8:34/Matt 16:24/Luke 9:23). Jesus' question to the two sons of Zebedee, after their mother had begged him to grant them a place on his left hand and on his right in his glory, points in the same direction: "Can you drink the cup that I drink or be baptized with the baptism with which I am being baptized?" (Mark 10:38; cf. Matt 20:22). And lastly there are Jesus' actions during his last meal with his disciples, as we shall see later, in his breaking and distributing bread and giving them the cup to drink; should one not understand them as, at the very least, actions that were meant to bind the disciples together with himself as he faced up to his imminent fate?

Quite obviously, sharing these tasks and roles with Jesus did not mean that his disciples were also taken up into the person of God. The more Jesus shares his status with his disciples and offers to share with them his way and indeed calls upon them to do so, the harder it becomes to speak of Jesus' uniqueness. There remains ultimately the fact that it is he who shares and offers all this in God's name, who made it possible then and still makes it possible. To do that, however, he does not need to be divine, but simply God's servant and messenger. Sharing this work with him was part of the reality of the life of those first disciples.

A "Son of Man"?

Jesus' avoidance of titles which would have distinguished him from the rest of his fellows is widely recognized, even if the use of one would not necessarily imply that he was divine or superhuman. Yet there remains his puzzling use of the phrase "son of man," at least sometimes seemingly in an oblique self-reference. To say that he refers to "*the* son of man" may, however, be misleading. For one thing, our distinction between a definite and an indefinite article may not have been such a clear-cut matter in semitic languages of the time, and even in Greek, as in English, the definite article could also be used generically (e.g., Wordsworth's "the Child is father of the Man," a general statement that he seeks to relate to his own experience; the use of capitals has, however, encouraged some to seek yet deeper meanings in the line). More significant, though, is the recognition that once Christians treated this phrase as peculiar to Jesus it took on a titular role that it had not possessed before. For them the phrase referred only to one person and to him alone. It may simply be that Jesus referred to *a* "son of man." But what then did he mean by the use of this phrase? It is not historically improbable when John has Jesus' hearers ask, perplexed, "Who is this son of man?"—incidentally, the only use of the phrase in the Gospels that is not on the lips of Jesus. (Otherwise there is Stephen's vision in Acts 7:56, but generally the phrase was little used in early Christianity, presumably largely because of its obscurity.)

A small group of sayings refer to the activity of a "son of man" on earth and these seem to refer to Jesus himself, but not necessarily solely to him. That has not prevented the rise of some parallel sayings where one version has "the son of man," the other the first person singular. One could seek to understand these as generic uses of the phrase with the definite article, but it is hard to make that work in every case. When we read that "the foxes have lairs and the birds in the air have nests, but the son of man has nowhere to lay his head" (Matt 8:20/Luke 9:58) then it should be clear that some do have a place to lay their heads, even if Jesus (and the itinerant group that accompanied him) did not. And "the son of man came eating and drinking" (Matt 11:19/Luke 7:34) is contrasted with the ascetic John the Baptist.

Many used to refer to the figure of "the son of man" in Daniel 7 as the explanation of this usage, and some still do so, but in fact the phrase does not occur there; it is instead "one like a son of man" (7:13) that we meet there, a human figure in contrast to the beasts revealed in the preceding part of the vision, who is then interpreted as representing God's holy ones, victorious at last (7:27). Nor does the phrase "son of man" occur as a title in other later texts that pick up the imagery of Daniel 7; the use of the phrase or others like it must be preceded by references to Daniel's vision to be intelligible, which is then picked up with references to "that son of man" or the like, thus serving to reinterpret Daniel's vision of this figure. In contrast, such a preparation for the use of the phrase is lacking in the Jesus-traditions, and sayings of Jesus that clearly seem to allude to the imagery of the Danielic vision are often, plausibly, thought to be secondary and later formulations.

What is puzzling is that in some sayings Jesus seems to refer to a future "son of man" who is distinguished from himself. This is particularly true of Luke 12:8, "But I tell you, whoever acknowledges me before other people will also be acknowledged by the son of man before God's angels," but the same holds good of sayings like Luke 11:30 and 17:24, 26. (This impression is a strong argument in favor of the authenticity of such sayings, given early Christians' conviction that Jesus was "the son of man.") If one reads "a son of man" here, then again we seem to have a human figure who is either judging or, as some suggest, bearing witness to the character of those who are being judged by God. That leaves it open who that figure is: is it really someone other than Jesus or does he leave his hearers with the possibility that it is he who will judge or bear witness? (It should be recalled that Jesus speaks of a future role of the twelve as judges over the twelve tribes of Israel—Matt 19:28/Luke 22:30.)

This openness seems to be characteristic of Jesus' use of "son of man." It is not a recognized title, and this has led to the suggestion that it is precisely for that reason that Jesus used the phrase, to avoid a familiar title such as "Messiah" and its various associations, and does so in such a way that one is unsure whether a single individual, the whole human race, or a certain group of human beings is being referred to in each case. At any rate, it is a phrase that stresses the humanity of Jesus and possibly others whom he associates with himself. Yet, despite this seeming avoidance of titles on the part of Jesus (and despite Matt 23:8–10!) this has not prevented many Christian traditions from building up multi-tiered hierarchical structures with prestige-laden titles. Both this and the metaphysical claims made for Jesus himself find little support in the Jesus-traditions, at least those of the first three canonical Gospels.

The reality with which we are left, then, is a this-worldly one and the figure of Jesus a thoroughly human one. But here, too, there is the question of the reality beyond this world, to which Jesus appealed and from which he derived his authority. For in *The God of Jesus* I argued, on the one hand, that Jesus' view of God seemed to encompass elements that are hard to reconcile with one another (gracious and merciful and forgiving and yet condemning, at least in a coming world) and, on the other, that the anthropomorphisms inherent in his way of talking of God were to be viewed with suspicion, as misleading and unsuited to our age and to any adequate conception of the divine. And when it came to the crunch it is hard to avoid the impression that this view of God, born of Jesus' age and its assumptions, was challenged and called in question by the manner of his lonely fate on a Roman cross. Christians today, looking to or for a reality beyond this world as justification for, and guide to, their way through this world, may well wonder how far it is adequate simply to appeal to this same God, or whether Jesus' God-concept also needs to be both stripped of much that was implicit in it then and also added to it in the light of subsequent theological and philosophical reflection. At any rate, there are various choices for those embarking on the Christian way. Some may well stick, more or less, with the traditional God of Jesus and the traditions of Jesus' teaching. Others will content themselves with the earthly Jesus and with at least some of the traditions concerning him, trusting that their wholly earthly pilgrimage may be recognized and justified by the ethical and social fruits that it bears rather than by any supernatural or metaphysical undergirding. Another group, however, while distancing themselves from the ideas of the divine nature current in Jesus' time and adopted by him, albeit selectively and perhaps not altogether consistently, are unwilling to abandon completely talk and conceptions of an "other" or a "beyond (this world)."

3

Following Jesus

The years that followed Jesus' birth are wrapped in obscurity. We have only the brief account in Luke's Gospel of the young Jesus engaged in discussion with Jewish scholars (2:22–39), an account that stands alone and, edifying though it may be, is therefore of questionable reliability from a historical perspective. This period in Jesus' life was a gap in our knowledge that obviously frustrated and fascinated some early Christians, leading them to compose highly imaginative accounts of the young Jesus, which we find amongst the New Testament apocrypha, stories that are decked with all kinds of miraculous features, some of them morally and theologically questionable.

Only with the accounts of Jesus' baptism by John the Baptist in the River Jordan do we regain the firm ground of history. Although the accounts of this may also include miraculous elements, especially the divine voice that speaks from heaven, it can only with difficulty be doubted that Jesus did in fact submit to John's baptism. For this was an account that posed problems for Jesus' followers later. In the first place, it seemed to make Jesus subordinate to John and, secondly, the fact that it was a baptism for the forgiveness of sins created difficulties as soon as one regarded Jesus as sinless, and that came about fairly early in the church's thinking about Jesus (cf. 2 Cor 5:21). (All the more striking then is the story of the rich young man who addresses Jesus as "good," only to be told that this adjective is only to be used of God: Mark 10:17-18/Luke 18:18-19; cf. Matt 19:17.) These difficulties in the account of Jesus' baptism have left their mark in some apologetic wriggles in the early Christian texts: so Matthew has John try to prevent Jesus from receiving baptism on the grounds that it should be the other way round, with John being baptized by Jesus. This is overruled by Jesus with the somewhat enigmatic saying that it is necessary thus to fulfill all righteousness (Matt 3:14-15). In the apocryphal gospel fragments we find the question of Jesus' sinlessness emerging. So the church father Jerome (*Adversus Pelagianos* 3:2) mentions a fragment of an early Christian gospel (which Jerome refers to as the Gospel of the Hebrews, used by the Nazarenes) where Jesus at first seems to demur at the idea of accompanying his mother and brothers to be baptized by John, on the grounds that he has no sins to be forgiven; yet perhaps, he adds, his reaction is itself a reason to go, a reply that is thought to mean that he is by his reaction revealing a sin of ignorance. This text is, however, also unusual in implying that Jesus was accompanied to the Jordan by his mother and brothers; for we find little evidence of this elsewhere and little sign, too, of such solidarity of his family with the actions of Jesus. Indeed, the somewhat vaguely formulated text of Mark 3:21 could be taken to mean that it was they who regarded him as crazy, although other interpretations have been suggested.

"Follow Me"—as a Wandering Missionary?

Wherever on the Jordan John was active, Jesus had to leave his home in Nazareth to come to him and the Gospels seem to suggest that from now on Jesus had little contact with his home town or his family. Mark 6:1–5 tells of one visit to Nazareth characterized above all by the refusal of most of those there to believe in Jesus' work. Luke 4:29–30 goes further and tells of an unsuccessful attempt to kill Jesus there. Jesus' base during the time of his ministry, if we can really speak of one, seems to have been elsewhere; for instance, in Capernaum.

For Jesus' life during this period seems to have been a largely itinerant one. To such a life, the Gospels tell us, he also called a number of followers, and obedience to this call meant considerable hardship and danger. If the life of most, if not all, of these followers had not hitherto been a particularly comfortable or secure one, from now on it was even less so. They would be dependent on finding sympathetic hearers as they travelled, sympathetic enough to offer them hospitality in the form of food and shelter and such other assistance as might be necessary or helpful, for instance for transport. Thus we read of the use of boats or of a donkey. But doubtless much of their travels they covered on foot. And it is very doubtful whether they were always successful in finding the help and support that they needed. The reception that Jesus apparently received in his home village, mentioned above, seems to suggest that there at least this support would not have been forthcoming. Thus when we read of Jesus' followers plucking ears of corn as they travelled (Mark 2:23/Matt 12:1/Luke 6:1), this should not be thought to be like picking wayside fruit on a stroll through the countryside, a tasty enhancement of the pleasures of the walk. It is likely, rather, that they were extremely hungry, so hungry as to care little about possible religious problems if they did this on the Jewish sabbath, and Matthew in fact states that they were hungry. The reality of an itinerant life was a harsh one. One must then presumably take with a pinch of salt the claim of Luke 22:35 that, when Jesus asked his disciples whether they had lacked for anything as they were sent out without a purse or bag or sandals, they could reply "Nothing." That is hardly to be expected, and the account of the disciples plucking ears of corn because they were hungry issues a note of caution. It is true that one could say that the good God had provided those ears of corn, even on the sabbath, but does that line of argument correspond to the likely reality of their situation or does it spring from wishful thinking? On the other hand, it is Luke that supplies a piece of information only mentioned later in the accounts of the crucifixion in the other Gospels, namely that Jesus' itinerant companions included women, and apparently, according to Luke, some well-endowed ones at that. In 8:1–3 we read that some women that had been healed by Jesus accompanied him and the twelve, and Mary of Magdala, Joanna, the wife of Herod's steward Chuza, and Susanna are named amongst a larger group; these ministered to them from their possessions. (In its account of those present at Jesus' crucifixion Mark 15:40–41 names Mary of Magdala and also Mary the mother of James the younger and of Joses, and Salome; Matt 27:55–56 also mentions Mary of Magdala, and also Mary the mother of James and Joseph, as well as the mother of the sons of Zebedee; Luke 23:49 mentions at this point that there were women from Galilee present, but omits the ministering and any names.) The ministering is mentioned by the other two Synoptic Gospels, but not the possessions, so that one could suppose that only things like cooking what others had given them or the like was involved. Luke's version presumably presupposes that some of them had money with them. (Is one to suppose that Mark 6:37 means that they would have had two hundred denarii at their disposal to buy bread for the crowd in the wilderness?) Thus, the harsh reality of their itinerant life may have been offset by natural resources (ears of corn), the hospitality of well-wishers, and such financial resources as they had with them. Nevertheless, it would take time before such support built up and natural resources would only be available at the appropriate season. Never lacking for anything still seems over-optimistic.

Often the expression "itinerant charismatics" or the like is used to describe this way of existence shared by Jesus and those who obeyed his call. Above all, this classification of Jesus and his followers is linked with the name of that innovative and versatile scholar, Gerd Theissen of Heidelberg, but the usage is widespread in scholarly circles, though not without qualifications as we shall see. Yet at first sight the description seems thoroughly apt, for Jesus and this circle of those that he had called to follow him were certainly "itinerant," wandering from place to place in Galilee and neighboring regions. And the healing activity practiced by Jesus and also his followers seems to justify the label "charismatic."

Yet it is difficult to link this sort of existence with that of most of those who would today name themselves followers of Jesus. For the lives of the great majority of those who call themselves "Christians" give a very settled, established impression; not only do they have homes in which they live, but often their branch of the Christian community has its own established and settled existence in the form of places of worship, offices, and in many cases other institutions such as schools, hospitals, and homes for the elderly and for orphans.

Again, one would hesitate to call a great many of these followers today "charismatic," at least in terms of the range of manifestations of charisma that what is known as "the charismatic movement" has singled out as its most distinguishing features, notably healing and "speaking in tongues." Yet one can apply the adjective "charismatic" far more broadly if one follows Paul's lead. For, confronted by the potentially divisive claims to possess the spirit voiced by some members of the churches that he had founded, particularly that at Corinth, he listed in his letters a range of activities that also came from God's spirit and contributed to the well-being of the church: whereas the list in 1 Corinthians 12:4–11 may strike us as bordering on, and similar to, gifts like healing and "tongues," Romans 12:6–8 offers a far wider and more "down to earth" list: while (intelligible) "prophecy" remains, the list goes on to mention "service," "teaching," "exhortation," "generous giving," "responsible leadership," and "cheerful compassion." In that sense, a great many members of the Christian church today, at least those playing some active role and contributing to its life, can also claim to be "charismatic."

Nor should one read the evidence of the Jesus-traditions as if it were only Jesus' itinerant followers that "followed" him, except in the narrower sense of a life of itinerancy. (If many Christians today still are prepared to speak of themselves as "followers" of Jesus then it is usually meant in a looser, wider sense.) Otherwise there is the danger that others could be viewed as second-class, as not properly obedient to Jesus' call. Sometimes the radicality of Jesus' challenge could give cause for that impression: the brief reference to a man who asked to go and bury his father before he obeyed Jesus' call and followed him is particularly striking; Jesus' somewhat enigmatic response that he should leave the dead to bury the dead seems to set aside a fundamental tenet of Jewish piety, the command to honor one's parents (Matt 8:21–22/Luke 9:59–60). However, Jesus' call as well as the example of his own life do seem to have involved leaving one's parents. The sons of Zebedee, too, must leave their father to attend to his fishing with the help of hired servants (Mark 1:20/Matt 4:22). This is sometimes put with a starkness that is to our ears repellent: Luke 14:26 even speaks of the need to "hate" one's family as well as one's own life (the following verse talks of the need to take up one's cross and follow Jesus) if one is to be Jesus' disciple. Apparently this harsh saying was too much even for Matthew's ears, for he tones it down (10:37): it is loving one's relatives more than Jesus that is condemned. This is offset according to Mark 3:35 by the creation of a new family consisting of all who do God's will. Nonetheless, it seems likely that in reality the call of Jesus was an uncomfortable business. I recall a discussion in a seminar in Cambridge where one of the professors, who was especially appreciative of Pasolini's depiction of the Gospel according to St. Matthew, was challenged by one of his colleagues on the grounds that it portrayed a Jesus who was lacking in humanity and basic human feelings. That may be true as an assessment of that film and yet I would hesitate to say that Pasolini had distorted what he had read in that Gospel. And if much of Jesus' ethical teaching bears the gentler marks of Jewish wisdom traditions, then there is another strand to his teaching with which we may well feel less comfortable, that comes to expression above all in his uncompromising "follow me" addressed to those who should leave everything and share his life of itinerant ministry, as well as in the strength of language with which he reproached his opponents and critics. Pasolini's film also gave a strong impression of what one might call a sort of fanaticism. Again, this is probably not something that this film-maker has made up, but it lies near to hand in the text of Matthew's Gospel and in what was probably the reality of such a life in those days and in that context.

Yet the response that Jesus desired was in at least one case expressly a refusal to let a would-be disciple take up an itinerant life: for the man healed of demon-possession in the district of the Gerasenes desires to accompany Jesus, but is told to go home and tell his own people what God has done for him; that commission he interprets quite widely, for he sets about preaching in the surrounding region of the Decapolis (Mark 5:18–20). In other words, he would possibly be of more use to Jesus' work staying in his home territory rather than crossing over to the other side of the Sea of Galilee. And in general it was important for the effectiveness of the itinerant mission of Jesus and his inner circle that they could avail themselves of the support and hospitality of sympathizers where they could find them. Only occasionally we do find hints of these places where Jesus and his disciples could expect to be received—the house of Simon Peter and Andrew in Capernaum, where Simon's mother-in-law lived (Mark 1:29–30/Matt 8:14/Luke 4:38) or the house in Bethany near Jerusalem, according to John the home of Martha, Mary, and Lazarus (11:1; cf. also Mark 11:11–12; Matt 21:17; but in Luke 10: 38–42 these two women are simply said to live in "a certain village"). Nevertheless, it is plausible to suppose that in many places there were those who had benefited from his ministry, physically or spiritually, and would be ready to do what they could for him. When, however, he or his disciples came to areas where they and their message were hitherto unknown it would be another matter, and Jesus prepared them accordingly for possible rejection: Mark 6:11; Matt 10:14–15; Luke 10:10–12. That could apply all the more as their work took them further afield into areas adjoining Galilee, into the territory of the tetrarch Philip (Mark 8:27/Matt 16:13) or the region of Tyre and Sidon (Mark 7:24/Matt 15:21).

The prominence and importance of this itinerant mission is to be found in Jesus' view of the very brief time available in which to make known God's will known and to manifest the outworking of God's kingly rule. He had to travel around himself and to involve others in an extension of his own work if anything more than a small handful of villages were to hear his message and to experience the impact of the arrival of God's kingly rule in the form of various works of healing. Even with the help of these itinerant fellow workers Jesus warns that they will not have completed their work in the towns of Israel before the "son of man" comes (Matt 10:23).

Yet it would be mistaken to suppose that this was demanded of all who heard Jesus' message and responded positively to it, although it is clear that for some a similar self-denial and a life as wandering missionaries continued on into the time after Jesus' death, as the Acts of the Apostles shows. That is true initially not just of the inner circle of the twelve, but also possibly, for instance, of some from the circle of the "Hellenists" (particularly if the Philip of Acts 8:5–40 is the one mentioned in 6:5 and is not the Philip found in the Synoptic Gospels' lists of the twelve and in Acts 1:13), and most notably of the apostle Paul and his co-workers.

It should be clear, however, that, if the expectation of an imminent end forms at least part of the basis for this radical call to follow Jesus, then this rationale has worn rather thin with the passage of time. It is true that down the centuries there have been those that have sought to whip up a comparable apocalyptic fervor, even daring to name the day on which the awaited end would come. One would have thought that the claim to know when the end would come (despite Mark 13:32/Matt 24:36) would have been discredited down the centuries as time after time the end was foretold and never came, but still one hears such claims made, although perhaps the voices of such self-styled prophets have become a little more muted. For the majority of Christians today the world goes on its way. There may be local catastrophes, either natural or caused by human evil in the form of wars or environmental irresponsibility or the like. Or, if there is a threatened global end of the world as we know it, then it in all likelihood approaches but gradually, helped on by such factors as the environmental irresponsibility just mentioned. However, precisely because its approach is gradual it is hard to arouse an active sense of responsibility, particularly in view of the number of competing vested interests that stand in the way of the needed responsibility.

A Way for Some or a Way for All?

Nonetheless, it seems clear that not all of the demands that Jesus made upon his hearers applied only to those that joined him in his itinerant life and mission. Yet it is a problem for those who wish to "follow" Jesus in the wider, looser sense just mentioned above to know what applied only to the itinerant sort of "following" and what was of wider relevance. Sometimes it will be clear: on the one hand, there are the instructions that Jesus gives to an inner circle of disciples as he sends them out as missionaries (e.g., Matt 10:5–16; Luke 9:1–5; 10:3–12). On the other hand the call to love one's neighbor is clearly meant for all, and all the clearer for being a commandment from the Old Testament (Mark 12:31/Matt 22:39/Luke 10:27; cf. Lev 19:18). There is also, for instance, the call to enter God's kingdom like a child (Mark 10:15), even if scholars are not agreed upon the characteristics of a child that are meant here; perhaps most probable is that child-like trust that Jesus himself manifested towards his God, even if at the last that trust seems to have faded as he accuses his God of deserting him (Mark 15:34/Matt 27:46). In Matthew 7:21 it is doing the will of that God that is the condition for entering the kingdom, rather than simply saying "Lord, Lord."

That will of God is hardly just the radical obedience and self-denial that was expected of those who, like Jesus, left everything in order to live as wandering messengers of God's kingly rule. And there was more to it than simply that trust in God just mentioned. That trust took concrete form in a way of life that was to be lived by all, also by those who were not called to leave their homes to spread the news of God's rule, and not just by those who followed an itinerant lifestyle. Much of the teaching bundled together in what we know as the Sermon on the Mount in Matthew 5–7 applies to both categories of disciples of Jesus; perhaps not everything there is equally applicable to both, but nevertheless has relevance for both.

At first sight, for instance, the injunction to take no thought for one's daily needs for food and clothing (Matt 6:25–34/Luke 12:22–32) might seem particularly appropriate in the case of itinerant charismatics. Yet the often precarious existence of a society such as that of rural Galilee, leading an existence of subsistence farming that was often hard enough at the best of times and became acute when times of drought or harvest failure were experienced, should not be overlooked. It is significant that a prayer for bread finds its place amongst the brief petitions of the Lord's Prayer (Matt 6:11/Luke 11:3; whatever the problems presented here by the rather enigmatic Greek adjective *epiousios*, which the early versions of the New Testament have variously struggled to translate, it is likely that Matthew's adverb "today" and Luke's adverbial phrase "daily" show that they understood this to refer to daily needs, rather than, say, a still future supplying of their needs). And again, if the form of the Lukan beatitude in Luke 6:21 is earlier than its Matthean equivalent (5:6) with its addition of "for righteousness," then this also attests the ever present threat of hunger amongst Jesus' hearers. This might be a particularly acute danger for his itinerant followers, but was not limited to them. At any rate, while some of the Beatitudes might have an even greater relevance for Jesus' closest followers, such as that for those persecuted, hated, and reviled (Matt 5:10/Luke 6:22), others seem to have a wider reference, perhaps even one extending beyond the ranks of those who believed in Jesus—the poor (especially if the "in spirit" of Matt 5:3 is secondary, in contrast to Luke 6:20's "poor"), the meek, the merciful, the pure in heart, the peacemakers.

Such a wider scope is the more likely if indeed some of the ethical teaching found here draws upon Jewish wisdom traditions. It is also likelier if we recall that God is also here described as causing the sun to rise on good and evil alike and sending rain on both righteous and unrighteous (Matt 5:45). It is fitting, then, that God's children, all of them and not just a select group, should love their enemies and pray for their persecutors (Matt 5:44).

Similarly, when Jesus speaks of forgiveness, God's forgiving us and our readiness to forgive our fellows, it is unlikely that this only applies to a limited circle of Jesus' followers. God's forgiving us is linked to our forgiving others (Matt 6:12/Luke 11:4; cf. Matt 6:14–15; Mark 11:25; Luke 6:37). This is illustrated graphically by the story told in Matthew 18:23–35: a king sells a slave who owed him ten thousand talents (an incredibly large sum, so that one wonders how a slave could possibly fall that far into debt) together with his wife and children and possessions, yet relents at the entreaties of the slave and remits the debt. When this same slave then goes and brutally seeks to extract the far smaller sum of a hundred denarii from a fellow slave and will make no allowance, the other slaves are incensed and tell their master, who cancels his previous act of leniency. The story ends with the threat that God will treat them similarly if they do not forgive their brothers or sisters from their hearts. This is told in response to the question posed by Peter as to how often they are to forgive their brothers; the answer is that seven times is not enough; rather it should be seventy times seven (Matt 18:21–22/Luke 17:4). That it is a matter of their relations with their brothers (and sisters) suggests that this instruction is for members of the Christian community (the New Revised Standard Version offers the interpretative translation "member of the church" in Matt 18:21), not just some of them, but all.

Jesus' contemporaries may therefore have been uncertain at times (but hardly on other occasions) how much of his ethical teaching applied to them if they were not amongst those following him in the narrower, literal sense. For those hearing these commands today there is an additional problem. For one should not imagine that the sort of ethical teaching found in the likes of the Sermon on the Mount is always directly applicable today. I recall hearing of a group of New Testament scholars crossing the Sea of Galilee; one of them tossed a toffee wrapper into the water, provoking the question "Would Jesus have done that?" and the retort "Jesus didn't have toffees." One may ask of such an exchange how seriously it reckoned with the self-denial demanded of Jesus and his itinerant companions, but then it was presumably not concerned with being serious at all, however considerable the hermeneutic problem on which it touches. And yet more seriously, one needs to ask whether the worldview projected by the Sermon on the Mount is not at many points rather too blandly positive. The rain that God sends can often be a blessing shared by righteous and unrighteous, but it can also be a curse that sweeps them both away alike as well, and the blessing of sunshine in the absence of rain leads to the curse of droughts. If there was a dark side to the blessings of nature then that is passed over in silence by this passage in the Sermon on the Mount, and this side has become even darker today; those following Jesus' teaching today will have to add other dimensions to the question of their relationship to the natural world than just those reflected in Jesus' own teaching. And the promise of God's provision of food and clothing in Matthew 6:25–34, even if it happened to have come true for the group of disciples travelling with Jesus then, is hardly one that has always been fulfilled for his followers since that time, let alone for the rest of humanity. And when Jesus tells his disciples to be "perfect" as God is perfect (Matt 5:48), then one may well ask how this is to be understood and whether it is at all realistic.

This stark demand for a God-like perfection sums up a fundamental problem of Jesus' ethical teaching that has puzzled Christians down the centuries: how does this demand correspond to any realizable reality, even realizable for the innermost circle of Jesus' followers, let alone for others? The picture that the Gospels paint of the lives of those disciples shows little sign of even an approximation to what could be called perfection: particularly in Mark's account their repeated failures of understanding (e.g., 4:13; 6:52; 7:18; 8:17, 21; 9:32), of love for one another (10:41), and at least a seeming lack of concern for their fellow human beings (6:35–6; 10:13) mount up steadily. And before one condemns them too severely, there is the problem of Jesus' own action in the Jerusalem temple; unless one downgrades this to little more than a very symbolic action, the other options suggested can include a very violent demonstration indeed or one coordinated with military action by militant Zealots, whose attitude to the occupying Romans and their collaborators was anything but loving. It should also be remembered that Jesus is represented as asking his followers whether they thought that he had been sent to bring peace on earth; not peace, he says, but a sword (Matt 10:34; Luke 12:51 tones down the violence of this somewhat by saying that Jesus brought "dissension"). It is true that one could discuss whether Jesus is talking of a consequence of his coming or its purpose, but it is likely that he would have viewed this as God's purpose rather than an unintended result. Nor can we say, unless we are to attribute all of the virulent and sharp invective and criticism of Jesus against his opponents to the hands of his followers, that Jesus himself always displayed a charitable and merciful tolerance of others' views. Much of it resembles John the Baptist's "you brood of vipers" (Matt 3:7/Luke 3:7) rather than the command to love one's enemies (cf. Matt 12:34; 23:33). Was all of this "perfection"?

What, then, was Jesus trying to articulate with his extremely radical ethical teaching and to whom did it apply? One approach has been to interpret his teaching in general as a two-stage ethic, with the more rigorous demands reserved for a spiritual elite (e.g., members of monastic orders) and a more relaxed ethic (but which?) for other followers. This leads inevitably to two corresponding classes of Christians. And, if Jesus' teaching applied to his own time, then the more rigorous teaching was reserved for his itinerant followers, so that again we have two classes of disciples. Rather different is the separation of the realm of officialdom and the state from that of the private person. Jesus' teaching would then bear upon the latter in all its stringency, but it is far from clear that Jesus was thinking of legislating for the state and its rulers at all. Others have sought to soften these demands of Jesus by making them a matter of attitude on the part of the individual, an attitude that can be summed up as love, rather any concrete fulfillment of the individual commands.

Others have found the clue in the very fact that these demands cannot in principle be fulfilled; confronted with them we discover our need for redemption. Or one could say that these demands are fulfilled for us by Jesus himself and by him alone (although we have just seen reasons for reservations in this respect). Or this ethic has been treated as one that is not to be fully realized in the present time, but in the world to come. In contrast there is the interpretation associated with the name of Albert Schweitzer, that this teaching is one of temporary relevance in the exceptional circumstances prevailing in the short time before the imminent end. Yet it would seem that for Jesus the kingly rule of God was already something present in Jesus' works of healing, so that what was appropriate to the end could not be separated so sharply from what was happening now.

Christians have thus wrestled with the problem what to make of Jesus' ethical teachings. Unfortunately Jesus does not seem to have posed the question whether his teachings could be fulfilled or not, or at least he has given us no clear answer. Should we come to terms with them, in good Lutheran fashion, by seeing them as undermining any claim to righteousness, then we have to be careful not to assume simply that this was Jesus' understanding as well. It may well be that Jesus had a vision of the will of God that he declared to his hearers without asking whether it could be fulfilled, simply because he believed this to be God's will.

A Way into and with God's People?

It may be appropriate to link Jesus' teaching on God's blessings of rain and sun given to the righteous and unrighteous alike with another prominent aspect of his life and ministry, namely his practice, evidently offensive to many of his religious contemporaries, of eating together with those who were social outcasts, the "sinners" in his world. He does not discriminate between righteous and unrighteous, any more than God does.

The offence lay presumably in the combination of Jesus' claim to be acting as God's messenger and agent of the coming of the kingly rule of God with his keeping such company, without even requiring of those who ate with him that they first repent and cleanse themselves of their unrighteousness. For in these meals and in this table-fellowship God's salvation and kingly rule found symbolic expression. At least since Isaiah 24:23 and 25:6 God's kingly rule and a festive meal had been linked together: Isaiah 24 had ended with the declaration of God's kingly rule on Mount Zion and chapter 25 went on to speak of a rich, festive meal for all nations on that mountain. Jesus' guests joined him in an anticipation of that banquet of the end time, and the status of his guests illustrates the saying of Jesus in Matthew 21:31-32, which was at one and the same time a promise for the rejected and a warning to Israel's religious elite: the prostitutes and tax collectors will enter God's kingdom before Israel's rulers, because the latter declined to hear John the Baptist's message and repent. Jesus' table-fellowship with these religious outcasts gave a vivid and concrete form to this word. These meals were both a this-worldly reality and a promise of what was to become a reality in the world to come. In the early church, however, there seemed to have been little emphasis on this symbolism of the future world in their communal meals, with the possible exception of the celebrations of the Lord's Supper, to which we will come in the next chapter. Yet even there it seems to be a matter, not of already eating and drinking with the glorified Jesus, but of looking ahead to a still future meal. And if such scenarios of the end time have anyway worn rather thin and empty for many today, then there may be little for it but to regard this saying in Matthew 21 as an apt commentary on the significance of the reality embodied in Jesus' meals with the outcasts of his society.

There are a few references in the Jesus traditions to these meals, mentioned above all because they were a cause of offence to Jesus' religious critics (e.g., Mark 2:16/Matt 9:11/Luke 5:30). To judge from the early chapters of Acts, communal meals were also an important part of the life of the community that came into being in Jerusalem after Jesus' death. At first the element of controversy so prominent in the Gospels is lacking there and only returns with the story of Peter and the non-Jew Cornelius in Acts 10–11. Similarly it is at the center of the dispute in the church of Antioch in Galatians 2, although it is hard to reconcile the wavering and backtracking of Peter described there with the overwhelmingly divine guidance through two complementary visions that led the apostle in Acts 10 to overcome his reservations and scruples about entering the house of ritually unclean non-Jews. Paul's account inspires more confidence as to its accuracy, but probably implies that from that point on there were two sorts of Christian communities, especially with regard to the table-fellowship that they practiced: there were communities that still adhered to Jewish ritual requirements, only admitting non-Jews that had adopted some measure of conformity to Jewish rules, and communities that welcomed non-Jewish "sinners" without demanding of them or their meals ritual purity according to Jewish law. The reality in these two types of Christian communities and their meals differed: the one type were essentially Jewish communities that differed from their fellow Jews in seeing Jesus as God's promised "anointed one" and following his commandments; for them, however, these commandments said nothing about breaking down the ritual barriers between Jew and non-Jew that related to table-fellowship. The other type had set aside these restrictions and welcomed non-Jews into their midst. One can see here in the Pauline communities an extension of that openness to the "sinners" of Jesus' Jewish world that was displayed in his table-fellowship, with the "sinners" now being, in the eyes of pious Jews, the non-Jews of the wider Greco-Roman world.

Another feature of the communal life of the earliest Christian community in Jerusalem was that they had all things in common (Acts 2:44; 4:32). On the one hand, this does not seem to have been something expressly enjoined by Jesus, or at least it has left no deposit in the gospel traditions; his commands about giving generously to those who ask it of them seems to have had in mind those who did not belong to their circle, as the instructions about responding to military requisitions shows (Matt 5:41—the Greek word used here is a technical term for this sort of requirement). And yet it may have been true at least of his itinerant followers and those who offered them hospitality and support in their work. Some have seen here in Acts the imprint of a Greco-Roman philosophical idea, that friends have everything in common, and this may have influenced Acts' terminology. Yet, if so, it is an ideal that also found its echo in various Jewish groupings of the time, such as the Qumran community or the Essenes. One should not be too skeptical with regard to this feature, for it is to be remembered that Jesus' followers now found themselves in a different situation to that of their itinerant ministry in Galilee. Some of them remained in Jerusalem for longer periods of time, but could not support themselves so easily by their trades (fishing, for instance, was not an option there). Only by a certain pooling of resources, even selling property elsewhere and contributing the proceeds to the Jerusalem community, as Barnabas did (Acts 4:36–37), could they support their existence in that city. Thus, this feature of the early church's life owes its *raison d'être* to the specific situation in which Jesus' followers found themselves due to their move from Galilee to this city, and is not to be regarded as a *sine qua non* of Christian communal existence, however much it has found its imitators in later Christian communities such as monastic ones.

Further light on the ethical implications of life in an early Christian community can perhaps be gleaned, if indirectly, from the scene in Matthew 25:31–46, in which the "son of man" sits in judgment over the nations. There judgment is meted out according to the way in which those concerned have treated "one of the least of my brethren." Now it is true that it is doubtful whether this stems from Jesus himself rather than a later Christian hand, and also that it is apparently a matter of how non-Christians have treated these brethren, who are most likely to be seen as members of the Christian community. Or, at least, it is *also* a matter of that, but does it not follow, *a fortiori*, that it also has important implications for the way in which Christians treat their fellow Christians? In other words, if anyone did so, then Christians should feed their hungry fellow-Christians and give them drink if they are thirsty, welcome them if they are strangers (as they might well be if they were itinerant and arrived in an unfamiliar place), clothe them if they have no clothes, visit them if sick or in prison. In the second century, the satirist Lucian of Samosata describes the ministrations of the Christians to the imprisoned Peregrinus, a Cynic turned Christian (*Peregrinus,* 12). Do we not see here a concrete example of what Paul expects within the "body of Christ," that if one member suffers, all suffer with that member (1 Cor 12:26)? And if he was conscious of such concrete implications then his indignation at the way in which the Corinthians celebrated the Lord's Supper is scarcely surprising: they proceed with their own meal without attending to the needs of those who do not have anything, so that the latter go hungry (1 Cor 11:21–22).

What could be and doubtless often was a reality within the early Christian community may, however, be more difficult to realize within the modern Western world. The sort of ministrations that Peregrinus enjoyed in prison would hardly be possible under a prison regime in the Western world today, even if they might have been still in the Western world in the nineteenth century. And such is the communal life of many Christian churches today that in many cases one wonders how much their members know about the bodily needs of their fellow members or feel under any obligation to do something about them. If they are into feeding or clothing anyone or visiting anyone in hospital or in prison, it is more likely to be outsiders who are not members of their Christian community. And in some cases members of that community would prefer that their needs should not be known to their fellow Christians. Or at least that is the implication that one could draw from the reality of the communal life that is found among many Christian churches today. Their members come together for services of worship and depart again, perhaps after shaking the hand of the priest or pastor at the door. Apparently it is often tabu in those services to mention for prayer or action the personal needs of individual members of that congregation. Frequently there is little more social interaction among its members. In other words, the reality found, at least in Western Christianity today, differs greatly from that attested in the earliest Christian churches. Following Paul's injunction that all members of Christ's body should share the suffering of each individual member and rejoice with anyone that rejoices may be correspondingly difficult to realize. Table-fellowship might be part of the answer, even if it is only a coffee-table (to start with), if it enables Christians to share news and views. If that is all, then it may fall far short of the ideals glimpsed in the early church and subsequently, but, to be realistic, the sensibilities and individualism of the Western world in which Christians find themselves today are also realities to be taken into account, even if not to be taken over without critical appraisal or unchallenged. Too much turning back of the clock may be impracticable, but both the realities of the past and of the present can and need to be questioned, and the latter in particular asked whether they should not learn from those of the past.

No Certain Way?

This chapter breathes, then, an air of uncertainty, an uncertainty born either of the reality of Jesus' life and work or of the nature of the various traditions that have left their mark on the Gospels and on the life of Jesus and his followers and on the early Christian community. We started off with the uncertainty with regard to those addressed by Jesus' teaching: were his commands for all or for a far smaller circle of those who literally followed him around Galilee and the neighboring regions and eventually up to Jerusalem on that fateful last visit? Or were some for all and others for some? And there was the uncertainty whether all of these teachings could stem from one and the same Jesus, for they seemed to represent very different traditions, for example, a generous, compassionate, and tolerant one or an austere and threatening one. And how many of them have any relevance for us? For not only do a great many of them presuppose a worldview that many of us would find hard to share, but the world in which Jesus lived and taught was in many ways very different to ours and presented different problems; it would be foolish to expect Jesus always to have offered answers to problems of our world. His teaching clearly called for a communal life, be that life one of a wandering group or of more settled communities, but, apart from the uncertainty regarding which teachings applied to which form of life, the subsequent history of the Christian church has revealed countless fault lines along which Christians have split from their fellows, both sides claiming to be the heirs of Jesus.

If much of Jesus' ethical teaching bears the marks of Jewish wisdom traditions, then there is that other strand to his teaching that we saw earlier and with which we may well feel less comfortable, that comes to expression above all in his uncompromising "follow me" addressed to those who should leave everything and share his life of itinerant ministry, quite apart from the threats posed to the disobedient and unfaithful in the life to come. I mentioned Pasolini's film earlier and I recall the strong impression that parts of it gave of what one might call a sort of fanaticism. Again, this is probably not something that this filmmaker has made up, but it lies near to hand in the text of Matthew's Gospel and in what was probably the reality of such a life in those days and in that context.

"Fanaticism," however, is not a quality that many in the Western world, at least, would commend. For it is a characteristic that many would associate today particularly with the self-sacrifice of those who blow themselves and others up and commit other brutal atrocities in the name of their religion and with those who teach them that it is God's will to do so. Naturally one would hope and expect that following Jesus would not take such forms, but the reality of the history of the Christian church teaches us that at times it was little different there. In the name of this Jesus and his God all sorts of barbarities have been perpetrated, not only on those of other faiths, but on fellow Christians, be it to convert or to root out supposed heresy or simply to impose a particular form of the Christian life. Nor should it be thought that this is just a matter of past history. Sectarian struggles are not wholly a thing of the past. Branches of the institutionalized church or factions within it have also all too often allied themselves with, and condoned, governments whose record on human rights, peace, and other issues seems very hard to square with the legacy of Jesus. Hierarchical forms of church government are often themselves responsible for gross breaches of the human rights of individuals within the church.

The ethical teaching and the inclusive practice of Jesus are, nonetheless, aspects of his life and work that, as already mentioned, have been found attractive by many, including many that would not call themselves Christians in the sense of belonging to the institution of the Christian church. It is all more regrettable, then, that that institution has so often fallen well short of the principles and the practice characteristic of Jesus' ministry. As I have just mentioned, horrendous acts of loveless cruelty have been and even still are performed, ostensibly in the name of Jesus and his God, and arguments over this or that doctrine or practice have fragmented the Christian church into scores of different traditions that insist on their own correctness and will not acknowledge the legitimacy of the point of view of the others. And yet there are nevertheless examples to be found within it where that life, that doing the will of God which

Jesus proclaimed, is lived out, at least in some measure, either by individuals or by groups or communities. In such instances one can speak of the reality of a following of Jesus. Now a parable of Jesus is told in Matthew 21:28–32 in which a father instructs his two sons to go and work in the vineyard. One says "No," but afterwards repents and goes; the other says "Yes," but does not go. The answer to Jesus' question as to which of them did his father's will is obvious, and Jesus then compares the penitent tax collectors and prostitutes that responded to the message of John the Baptist with his hearers who had not done so. One could formulate this parable in terms of doing the father's will in reality and deceiving or deluding oneself in thinking that one was doing it.

Yet the way that Jesus himself trod and the example that he has given us is hardly unambiguous and we must rid ourselves of the insipid picture of "gentle Jesus, meek and mild," for none of those epithets really fit him at all. And the recognition of that does confront us with a dilemma: whoever Jesus meant to follow his way—an inner circle of disciples or all who received his message, or sometimes the one, at another time the other—can we endorse his way for ourselves or for our time? Or are we forced to be selective, to commend Jesus here and to criticize him there? Schweitzer, as we saw above, treated Jesus' teaching as applicable (but also with realistic prospects of fulfillment?) for a brief time before the imminent end. For his own day he spoke rather vaguely of the "spirit of Jesus," but even that "spirit" suffers from the ambivalence that beset Jesus' conduct and leaves us with a choice to make: which aspects of Jesus' teaching and conduct provide us with that "spirit" that should guide us?

Some of Jesus' teaching is beyond any reasonable doubt authentic and directed to all who hear him: in that category belong his commands to love God, one's neighbor, and even one's enemy, even when, as we saw, some of Jesus' utterances are surprising manifestations of that love if they are really that. With other teaching, even when we can be reasonably sure that it goes back to Jesus, it may be less certain whether it is meant for all or only for a select group of followers with a special mission. And there is then the further question how far it is applicable to our day and our circumstances. Paying one's workers the same wage regardless of how long they had worked for it (Matt 20:14) may illustrate a point about God's way of treating us, but cannot serve as a basis for modern industrial relations.

Nevertheless there is a certain consistency between some of Jesus' views of God and some of his ethical teaching and this may serve as a basis for tracing a way that his disciples should follow. I say only "some of Jesus' views of God" since I have already argued that the mercy and goodness that shows themselves in blessing just and unjust alike are hard to square with the threat of damnation left hanging over sinners in the world to come. Alongside that goodness and mercy available also for sinners we may set the readiness of Jesus to enter into fellowship with the sinners of his world. And if Jesus' God is a forgiving God, then it is only consequent that his followers are expected to forgive freely and generously and to form a community that is based on those qualities.

4

Remembering the Death of Jesus

Most branches of the Christian church, though not all, include among their practices some form of re-enactment of Jesus' last meal with his disciples, a meal overshadowed by the danger confronting him and them in Jerusalem, where Jesus' religious opponents held sway and whose hostility could only have been increased by the action that Jesus had taken shortly before within the Jerusalem temple itself. Exactly what he had done and what it meant may be debatable, but it can only have increased the priestly aristocracy's conviction that Jesus' movement was a threat to their power and position. There are various accounts of this meal and of the words spoken by Jesus then, but one of these, often that found in the earliest account, in 1 Corinthians 11:23–26, is used as the basis for an interpretative re-enactment of the meal. There are, too, Christian traditions that treat this occasion as a re-enactment, not just of the meal, but of Jesus' saving death, often involving a supernatural transformation of the bread and wine used into Christ's body and blood. In doing so a saving significance is attached to participation in the meal or the rite that it has become and a corresponding power and authority to those who are authorized to administer this.

It seems clear enough that Jesus held a last meal some time before his death, but our certainty about what really happened then ends about there. Traditionally he held this meal in an upper room in Jerusalem with the inner circle of his disciples, but even some aspects of this have been questioned. More important is the uncertainty about what he actually did and said on that occasion. For the traditions about this are divided and varied. With regard to the sayings spoken concerning the bread and the wine, the tradition found in Matthew and Mark is to be distinguished from that found in 1 Corinthians 11 and in the longer text of Luke. (For a shorter version of the witness of this Gospel also exists, in that a few witnesses omit the parallel in Luke to most of the well-known words in the Pauline version. The significance of this variant has perhaps been underestimated, for it is very hard indeed to see why, once the Pauline formulation was in the text of Luke, anyone should wish to delete it; its absence, on the other hand might seem to cry out to any scribe familiar with the Pauline tradition to be made good.) A standard conservative reaction to such variations in the gospel traditions is to assert that Jesus said something similar on different occasions but not quite the same thing, but that will not work with something like a last meal, which by definition cannot be repeated. In addition to these variations, the Fourth Gospel concentrates on Jesus' washing of his disciples' feet, although something reminiscent of his interpretative words over bread and cup is found in a completely different context in chapter 6, following on the miraculous feeding of five thousand and Jesus' declaration that he is the bread of life. The reference in another early Christian document, the *Didache*, to the last meal (9:1–4) is unusual in that it does not connect its version of the tradition with Jesus' death nor even locate its origin in the context of the passion of Jesus.

The question of the context also arises amongst those accounts that relate this tradition to Jesus' passion. A few references in the Gospels suggest that this meal was the traditional Jewish Passover meal (Mark 14:12, 14, 16/Matt 26:17–19/Luke 22:7–8, 11, 13) and this has been endorsed enthusiastically by some, a decision that can play an important role in the interpretation of what is happening and what is meant. Confirmatory evidence has been seen in features of the accounts, such as the fact that the meal had to be held in Jerusalem, that it was held at night rather than late in the afternoon, and that Jesus did not leave the city boundaries afterwards.

On the other hand, there is a series of counter-arguments, in part based on the accounts of the meal, in part on historical, above all chronological, considerations. The words of interpretation are spoken during the meal and not before it, as was the standard practice at a Passover meal, and they do not take the form usually employed at the Passover meal, in which the question would be posed as to the meaning of distinctive elements of that meal such as the unleavened bread or the bitter herbs, and the father of the household would then provide an interpretation based on the founding events of the feast on the eve of Israel's exodus from Egypt. We cannot be certain that the bread that Jesus broke and interpreted differed from normal bread in that it was unleavened. And, even if the drinking of wine was uncommon, it is striking that there is no reference in these accounts of the meal to the Passover lamb that was eaten on this occasion. It seems that a single, shared cup was used, not the individual cups associated with Passover. And, whereas the Passover meal was traditionally a family affair, there is no mention of the presence of any relatives, despite the tradition that some of them were in Jerusalem and witnessed Jesus' crucifixion, although admittedly it could not be expected of an itinerant band that they could on this occasion easily gather all the families that they had left behind in Galilee in order to follow Jesus.

Yet it is perhaps the historical and chronological difficulties that arise when it is assumed that this was a Passover meal that weigh more heavily. In the Fourth Gospel Jesus dies on 14 Nisan, *before* the time of the Passover meal; he dies at about the time of the slaughter of the Passover lambs in the Jerusalem temple, a timing that could have symbolic significance (as 1 Corinthians 5:7 shows) and that could therefore have been chosen by this evangelist for this purpose. More important is the fact that this chronology means that Jesus died before the beginning of the festival and that this removes a number of the difficulties in accepting the Gospels' accounts of the trials of Jesus and their legality. At any rate, Jewish judicial measures taken against Jesus before the feast would be a less glaring offence against Jewish custom and legal practice than would have been the case once the feast had begun. The most that one can say is that the Gospels may imply a trial before the beginning of the feast, and the same would be true of a further point, that Simon of Cyrene was coming in from the fields as Jesus was led out to be crucified (Mark 15:21).

Yet, even if Jesus did not celebrate the Passover meal itself, it is hardly to be doubted that it took place during the Passover season, in the period immediately before the feast itself, and that therefore the significance of the feast would be very much in the minds of Jesus and his disciples, even if the meal described in the New Testament accounts contained the characteristic features of festive Jewish meals in general and none of the really distinctive features of the Passover meal. It was a time of lively expectations, above all of messianic expectations in the broadest sense, as the people recalled God's rescue and deliverance of Israel in the past and would be encouraged to hope for another act of God to rescue them from their present subjection to foreign rule. For again and again we read that this feast was the occasion for demonstrations and rebellious acts, and that the Roman governor therefore felt obliged to take up residence in Jerusalem at this time, together with military reinforcements for the garrison there. In itself the massive crowds of pilgrims would have made that prudent, regardless of the religious associations of the festival. Therefore both the Jewish and the Roman authorities had good cause to be apprehensive when faced with the expectations that many of the people harbored with respect to Jesus' person and role.

Yet how far did the expectations and the symbolism of this feast affect the form and the nature of Jesus' last meal? For we have seen the silence of the accounts about the central elements of this meal such as the lamb or distinctive elements like the bitter herbs, and it is not easy to find allusions to the Passover feast in the words attributed to Jesus. As we have seen, for instance, those words lack the question and answer form typical of interpretative commentary on the elements of the meal. At any rate, whether it was a Passover meal or not, it was not the distinctive elements of a Passover meal that Jesus apparently found it appropriate or important to interpret. Above all, there is not the slightest hint that he identified himself in any way with the Passover lamb or any lamb at all in the manner either of 1 Corinthians 5:7 or that implied by John 1:29 and 19:36.

The Meaning of Jesus' Words?

Rather Jesus' words are concerned with bread and wine, but quite what his words were in this case is most uncertain. Later hands have added to them and altered them, and many scholars despair of ever knowing what, if anything, was originally said on this occasion. Yet one can judge it to be likelier, for a start, that material would have been added rather than deleted, unless there was something deemed offensive in it. That would mean, for instance, that when Mark has Jesus say of the bread just "take (it); this is my body" (14:22) this may well be earlier than versions which add "eat" (Matt 26:26) or "which is given for you" (Luke 22:19) or "for you" (1 Cor 11:24).

Another possible criterion is the presence or absence of parallelism, particularly in a text in regular liturgical use as Jesus' followers later re-enacted this meal. For Mark and Matthew have an answering word, parallel to "this is my body," over the wine, "this is my blood . . ." (Mark 14:24/ Matt 26:28), whereas the longer text of Luke and Paul have "this cup is . . " (Luke 22:20/1 Cor 11:25). The parallelism of "body" and "blood" is clear, but some have tried to argue that the idea of drinking Jesus' blood was so offensive that it was replaced by speaking of the cup: yet speaking of eating Jesus' body would surely have seemed just as repugnant and yet it remained.

Both these main strands of the tradition go on, however, to speak of a covenant, a concept that had hitherto been singularly absent from Jesus' teaching, but they seem to reflect a different background behind the use of the term. Matthew has "this is my blood of the covenant, which is shed for many for the forgiveness of sins" (26:28) and Mark "this is my blood of the covenant, which is shed for many" (14:24), and most see in these an echo of the rites described in Exodus 24: Moses reads the "book of the covenant" and the people promise obedience; Moses then splashes the people with the sacrificial blood of oxen and says, "See the blood of the covenant that the Lord has made with you in accordance with all these words." First Corinthians and the longer text of Luke's version allude instead to Jeremiah's promise of God's coming "new covenant" with Israel (31:31): "This cup is the new covenant in my blood" (1 Cor 11:25) and Luke adds to this "which is shed for you" (22:20).

Perhaps it would be wrong to ask which of these two traditions concerning the cup of wine was the earlier. After all, the presence of "this is my body" would have been enough to provoke the creation of matching sayings regarding the cup of wine. Moreover, there was another saying concerning the wine that is widely regarded as containing early tradition: "From now on I will not drink of the fruit of the vine until God's kingdom comes" (Luke 22:18), and "From now on I will drink of the fruit of the vine no more until that day when I drink it anew in God's kingdom" (Mark 14:25; Matt 26.29 adds a "with you" and reads "in the kingdom of my father"). To be added to this is the observation that the longer text of Luke as it stands contains two sayings about the wine, of which this is the first, preceded by a blessing which is only at best implicit before the second saying in verse 20, whereas the equivalent of this cup saying follows the sayings about the bread and wine in Matthew and Mark. And significantly this saying is a statement, whether it is a prediction or, as some suggest, a vow, that does not seem to attribute any saving role either to Jesus' death or to the drinking of the cup: it suggests that Jesus' death is near at hand, but it would take little prophetic skill to recognize that this was possible, even probable, given the situation in which Jesus now found himself.

If this cup saying said nothing about the cup as a means of, or pointer to, salvation, what of the saying about the bread? At first sight the statement "this is my body" looks like a straightforward identification of the bread with Jesus' body, in some sense or other, but the Greek word for "bread," *artos*, is masculine whereas the demonstrative pronoun "this," *touto*, is a neuter. This has led to the suggestion that what is identified with the body (or simply Jesus' "person"?) is the whole action of breaking, distributing, and eating the bread. This could come very near in sense to the collective sense of "body of Christ" that Paul uses, particularly in the context of the Lord's Supper in 1 Corinthians 10:16–17. It also points in the same direction when the theme of "covenant" is then later introduced as an interpretation of the shared cup. In this shared action a solidarity of community is established, by actions as much as words, between Jesus and his disciples, even if that solidarity is short-lived, as they will that very night leave him alone in the hands of those who have come to arrest him in Gethsemane.

In short, it may be suggested that neither what Jesus originally said about the cup nor what he said in connection with the sharing of the bread offer us an interpretation of the meaning of his death. It is near, and beyond it lies God's kingly reign, but Jesus must have been aware of the possibility of a violent death ever since John the Baptist had died at the hands of Herod Antipas. As I argued in *The Death of Jesus*, Jesus may have spoken of his fate being in the succession of Israel's prophets who had suffered at the hands of their fellows, but there is little secure evidence for further interpretative commentary on that death, nor does Jesus' agonized prayer in Gethsemane or the reluctance of his disciples to admit of the possibility, let alone the necessity, of his death, or Jesus' reproachful cry on the cross suggest that they saw it as salvific. And, as Gethsemane follows hard upon that last meal, it is unlikely that at that very moment Jesus had disclosed a hitherto unmentioned way of salvation that would be, could only be, opened up by his death. Those implications of his coming death would hardly have been forgotten so soon.

The Gospels tell of this last meal and Jesus' actions and words at it in the course of the story of his passion. Paul, on the other hand, sets his account in a different context, the later worship of the early church. In all probability elements of his account have been added to the account to adapt it to this different context: "do this in memory of me" and "do this, as often as you drink it, in memory of me"; "for as often as you eat this bread and drink from this cup, you proclaim the Lord's death until he comes" (1 Cor 11:24–26). These are likely to be later additions to the tradition, for Jesus may have expected one who was to come, but did not use "Lord" of himself, and it is doubtful how far he was concerned to regulate the future life of his followers in this way. At any rate, the world has continued far longer than he ever expected, and many of his followers still regularly re-enact this final meal with its words and actions, some of them undoubtedly still looking ahead to a coming of their Lord; for countless others, however, that expectation has faded and would be viewed by them as outmoded and no longer relevant. Similarly, the various theories of the atonement suggested by the different sayings about the bread and the cup (or which can be read into them) for many no longer match their view of God and God's dealings with, and relationship to, humanity. The imagery of blood-sacrifice, substitution, and the like is foreign to them, something unreal. Notions of some redeeming transaction between God and Jesus as our representative, and the assumptions about the nature of God implicit in these—e.g., that the justice or the wrath of God must be satisfied or placated—are ones that many Christians can no longer accept. And that raises the question of the reality that is now experienced in remembering and recalling the death of Jesus in this way.

We saw earlier how the community of the followers of Jesus was a reality in our world today, and the celebration of this meal expresses that solidarity more or less effectively, depending upon the form that that celebration takes in a particular community or strand of Christian tradition. It has its focal point in the past, although some forms of the liturgy seek to preserve the looking forward to a second coming of Jesus in the end time, however little this hope is a reality in the expectations of many of the worshippers. The looking back to the last meal and the imminent death of Jesus that overshadowed it provide a more secure focal point. For not only was that death a harsh reality, but it was, at least in a sense, "for many" or even "for us." But not necessarily in the sense of some theory of atonement, some transaction between Jesus and God, but rather in the sense that it was the outcome of a ministry proclaiming Jesus' sense of God's message to humanity, the message of a gracious and merciful God who is "for us." That message Jesus proclaimed to the end, even in the dangerous surroundings of Jerusalem at festival time, in the midst of his powerful enemies, so that as many as possible of God's people might hear his words. One may ask whether he could not have slipped away before things got too hot and have lived on to preach his message again, but in the end he did not, and he paid for his determination and commitment with his life. At least in that sense, then, his death was "for us," and the re-enactment of his last meal is a reminder of that commitment and self-sacrifice, calling us to a similar commitment and self-sacrifice for the sake of our fellows.

5

Living the Resurrection of Jesus?

The accounts of the appearances of the risen Jesus to his disciples have much in common with those relating to his birth. Both sets of accounts have been embellished in the interest of theological reflection: in the one case, above all in the doctrine of the incarnation of God; in the other, in the light of questions about the status and nature of Jesus now and about the nature of the world to come. In both cases, too, many of the details of the accounts differ and are hard to reconcile with one another, a problem exacerbated in the case of the resurrection appearances by the fact that we here have the version given by all four Gospels and not just two, as well the accounts offered by Paul's First Letter to the Corinthians and Acts' accounts of the appearance of the risen Jesus to that apostle. The differences in smaller details are many (e.g., which women visited the tomb and whom did they see there?), but there are weightier differences. For a start, there is the question of the location of the appearances, particularly when Luke has Jesus expressly instruct the disciples not to leave Jerusalem (24:49). That may be theologically motivated, but there is the important point that, if any of those who had accompanied Jesus to

Jerusalem were to see the risen Jesus on that first day of the week, it would have to be in or near Jerusalem. There simply would not have been time to reach Galilee again so soon after the crucifixion, especially in view of the Sabbath restrictions on travel. And yet a number of the other accounts mention or presuppose appearances in Galilee (Mark 16:7; Matt 28:16; John 21).

Even more serious is the matter of the nature of the appearances, and correspondingly that of the risen Jesus. Paul sets his own experience of the risen Jesus in the same sequence as those of the other, earlier witnesses whom he lists in 1 Corinthians 15:5-8, but when the writer of Acts comes to describe what happened to Paul on the way to Damascus, it is a matter of a heavenly vision, at times to Paul alone, at times shared in part by his companions. Yet the Gospels describe encounters with a figure that are no visions in heaven, but seem to be with a this-worldly human being—of some sort or other. For the British edition of *Beyond Resurrection* I had on the front cover Rembrandt's drawing of Jesus and the two disciples on the way to Emmaus (Luke 24:13-27). There the two disciples are being overtaken by a glowing, incandescent figure, yet when he catches up with them in Luke's account they seem to notice no difference between this stranger and any other human being. It is only later, symbolically, when they share a meal, that the penny drops and they realize who it was that had been with them (24:31). Again the risen Jesus is at first mistaken for a gardener by Mary of Magdala in John 20:15, but she then recognizes him when he addresses her by name. The male disciples, on the other hand, are confronted by one still showing the wounds of his crucifixion (John 20:20; cf. v. 25; Luke 24:39). Nonetheless Jesus seems able to pass through closed doors (20:19, 26), and it is therefore the more understandable when the disciples at first suppose him to be a ghost (Luke 24:37). That was presumably one reaction to the stories of the resurrection appearances, which Luke now wants to counter by insisting on the bodily reality of the Jesus who stood in their midst (24:38–43).

The variety of these accounts leave us with the impression that it is quite uncertain what the nature of the Jesus who appears to them really is. Paul does not greatly help us when he discusses the nature of resurrection existence in 1 Corinthians 15. That is regrettable, for he is, after all, in all probability the only New Testament writer who can himself claim to have seen the risen Jesus (15:8; cf. 9:1). Confronted by Corinthians who deny the resurrection of the dead, he insists that the nature of the resurrection existence is of a different kind to that of earthly existence and that our earthly nature cannot inherit God's kingdom, but must first be changed (15:37–57). Since the experiences of Jesus, the archetypal human being of the end time, the Adam of the end time (1 Cor 15:45), serve Paul as the model (the "first fruits," v. 20) for our existence in the world to come, it is to be presumed that what he here asserts of redeemed humanity was already true in Jesus' case too. In that case it is clear that he wishes to distinguish sharply between this-worldly human nature and that of the world to come (vv. 42–44).

Neither the gospel accounts nor Paul's assertions, taken together, offer us a clear picture of what happened to Jesus after his death nor of the postmortal existence awaiting the rest of us. For the Gospel accounts point in different directions and suggest different possibilities. Paul clearly insists that the new existence is different from the old: his stress on discontinuity contrasts with the concern of many Jewish texts and practices to stress an element of continuity (e.g., the preservation of the bones of the dead to provide the basis for a future resurrection). However, it should be noted that today some more progressive traditions of

Judaism have abandoned this form of expectation for a life after death and have indeed shifted their attention away from the life to come in order to concentrate on the present one. At any rate, the wisdom of a lifestyle based on the conviction that this life is (simply) a preparation for another life beyond death and the grave seems open to question. For the basis of that conviction is hedged about with altogether too many "ifs" and "buts" to seem reasonable. And if such a conviction serves to distract from the living of this life and from living up to its responsibilities and challenges, then this conviction is not worth the price and is to be regarded as a dangerous delusion. The alternative to belief in another life is, however, not what Paul scathingly dismisses as "Let us eat and drink, for tomorrow we die" (1 Cor 15:32). For Paul's message for this life (and also that of John too, though his language is rather different) is, as we shall see below, in fact an ethically and spiritually stringent and challenging one: we are to die to ourselves and find our life precisely in this death within this world. *Here and now* we will meet our God and live for our God.

The theoretical and conceptual possibility or impossibility of such a continuity between our bodily existence in this world and a form of existence in the world to come is, at any rate, a question that has exercised many philosophers. This question is one that is posed in a more concrete and tangible form by the varying accounts of Jesus' resurrection appearances. If the risen body was the old one, even with the wounds of his crucifixion still visible, why did some fail to recognize him? And what happened to Jesus between his resurrection appearances? Did he remain on earth and, if so, where and how? What about the visionary appearances such as that to Paul on the way to Damascus? For Paul himself seems to suggest that the risen Jesus had a qualitatively different body; is that not problematic if our bodies are essential for our identity as persons?

As a result it is unclear what really happened at Easter or will happen to us after our deaths. That reality eludes us. What is clear is that the disciples came to believe that they had seen the risen Jesus (evidently after some understandable hesitation in many cases; cf., e.g., Matt 28:17; John 20:24–25). How such a belief might have arisen has been explained in various ways, ranging from the traditional explanation that they had indeed seen Jesus alive again (but in what form?) to far more skeptical and dismissive suggestions. Whatever it was evidently sufficed to launch them once more on the way of discipleship.

From Paul's assertions about the centrality of the resurrection for Christian belief in 1 Corinthians 15 one would gain the impression that belief in such a resurrected life (in some form or other) was a *sine qua non* for this way of discipleship. Without it there would be no point in, or motivation for, this costly way. "If Christ has not been raised, then your faith is in vain, you are still in your sins . . . . If we have set our hopes on Christ for this life alone, then we are the most wretched of all people" (15:17, 19). Actually, Paul seems to be carried away by his own rhetoric at this point, since we would surely not want to deny the intrinsic worth and value of Paul's life or that of Jesus irrespective of the question whether or not they went on to be raised from the dead.

Resurrection Now?

However, there are also passages in which Paul speaks of a reality of resurrection life *in the present*, however paradoxical that may seem. And the paradoxical nature of what he is asserting needs to be emphasized, for it is true that the apostle also had to play down some Christians' over-inflated assessments of their spiritual present, especially in the Corinthian church. His exasperation and indignation bursts out in 1 Corinthians 4:8, where he ironically comments on the claim of some in that community to consider themselves already "filled," "rich," and "kings." And the whole thrust of his argument in the second part of 1 Corinthians 15 is also to the effect that the Corinthians were deluding themselves if they believed that their present, earthly existence could ever be their final state; first the final enemy, death, must be defeated (v. 26) and they must not confuse their natural existence in the image of the earthly man, Adam, with the nature of the existence that will be theirs in the image of the heavenly Adam of the end time, Christ (especially vv. 44–50).

Yet, while Paul does use the language of life and death, particularly in Romans 6, in a way that suggests that life is only attainable by passing through death—even if it is death "with Christ," whether that death with Christ takes place on Golgotha or in baptism or (as seems to me most likely) in both—he does at times also use the language of "life" and "death" rather differently. Even if some of the Corinthians might have used the language of "resurrection" of their present spirit-filled existence (which Paul would presumably have regarded as a seriously misleading misuse of language—"resurrection" is for him something that happens to the human body after death) or at least considered a future resurrection superfluous in the light of what they already enjoyed, Paul does not, but shows no such restraint with regard to the term "life." Dealing in Romans chapter 6 with the view of the critics of his message that being saved through grace meant that one was free to go on sinning, thus giving grace more scope (!), he argues that this is impossible, not only because Christians share in Christ's death to, and therefore break with, sin, but also because the purpose of their sharing in Christ's resurrection is that they might "walk in newness of life" (6:4). It is true that he does not expressly refer to their previous condition as "death," as his successors do in Colossians 2:13 and Ephesians 2:1, but the implication lies near at hand. (To express himself thus would be difficult, as he uses an apparently similar expression and construction with a very different sense: "dead to sin" means that one is delivered now from the power of sin (singular), in contrast to one's previous state.) In the following verses he has a future life with Christ in view as well, but, having spoken of Christ's own death with regard to sin and his life to or for God (6:10), he then goes on to call the Roman Christians to consider themselves dead with regard to sin, but living for God (6:11). To consider themselves in this way is no make-believe, but an appraisal of what their position actually is "in Christ Jesus." Similarly the word "walk" in 6:4 not only clearly suggests that he is referring to their present existence and conduct in this world. Indeed the whole thrust of his argument here demands that he address the issue of Christians' conduct here and now, in order to rebut the suggestion that his message means that Christians may persist in sin to give grace more scope (6:1). So, although he may be critical of the Corinthians for their exaggeratedly "realized eschatology," he does not eschew all anticipations of the end, the eschaton, in the present. In particular, the gift of God's spirit to Christians is a foretaste, an anticipation, a "pledge" or "down-payment" for the future age here and now (2 Cor 1:22; 5:5), a "first fruits" of what is to come (Rom 8:23), just as Christ's resurrection was in his eyes the "first fruits" of a still-future resurrection (1 Cor 15:20). Thus it is characteristic of Paul's thought that for him Christians live as ones already having, but at the same time not yet having, the future state, and Christian existence is marked for him by this tension between these two poles of the already fulfilled and the not yet fulfilled.

Thus in Paul's thought we find not only the theme of "life through death," as in his treatment of baptism "with Christ" in Romans 6, but also that of "life in death." This paradoxical idea is particularly prominent in 2 Corinthians. There the apostle speaks of "constantly carrying about in our body the putting to death of Jesus, in order that Jesus' life might be revealed in our body. For we who are alive are constantly being delivered up to death for Jesus' sake, in order that Jesus' life might be revealed in our mortal flesh" (4:10–11). This is seemingly a resurrection life manifested, not in leaving death behind or escaping from it, but precisely in the bearing of it. It is true that Paul does not here speak of "resurrection," but of Jesus' "life" being manifested in us. "Resurrection" was for the ex-Pharisee Paul so much a matter of postmortal existence that he probably could not bring himself to speak here of "resurrection." (Those followers of his who probably wrote Colossians and Ephesians did not shrink from speaking of Christians having been *raised already* with Christ: Col 2:12; Eph 2:6.) However, had the apostle himself been prepared to use the word metaphorically, it would have been an apt way to describe the power that enables us to surmount the "death," physical and spiritual, that threatens us in this life, that power that enables us to have "life" despite that threatening "death." Of his apostolic ministry the apostle similarly affirms that "we are dying and, look, we are alive" (6:9); this remark is found amidst a series of paradoxical antitheses in 6:8–10 which are somewhat reminiscent of those found earlier in 1 Corinthians 7:29–31. Such paradoxes were beloved of popular philosophy of the time, but this particular paradox is stated by Paul with a sharpness unparalleled in extant Greco-Roman literature of the period. Perhaps one should not expect that parallels were to be found easily, because to conclude that true life was to be found in death might seem to encourage martyrdom or suicide as its logical consequence. Paul, however, is not speaking primarily of his own martyrdom, even when that perhaps threatened him and seemed very near (1 Cor 15:31-32; 2 Cor 1:8), for it was of decisive importance for him and for his understanding of his own existence that he was caught up in, involved in, Christ's death, and he could even say that he had died with Christ on the cross and that he therefore, like Christ, lived to and for God (Gal 2:19; cf. Rom 6:10). That was for him determinative, not what in fact happened to his own physical body.

If the form of Paul's paradoxical language has its analogies in popular philosophy of the time, another tradition has in all probability also made its influence felt—the early Christian tradition of Jesus' teachings. For the ideas expressed here are close to those sayings of Jesus that speak of losing one's life and gaining it and *vice versa* (Matt 10:39; 16:25-26; Mark 8:35-36; Luke 9:24-25; 17:33; John 12:25); even if the gaining or losing of life were originally meant or could be understood to be something that lay in the future, these sayings are sometimes also formulated in the present tense (cf. John 12:25a; also 12:24 and Mark 8:36) and the futures of the remaining ones could easily have been interpreted as logical rather than temporal ones: the one who loses his life now will, in so doing, gain it and gain it now.

The celebration of Easter has been, and still is, heavily overlaid with a triumphalism that seems hard to reconcile with the fragility and uncertainty of the traditions of Jesus' resurrection appearances and with the subsequent uncertainty of what awaits us all beyond death. Indeed, it has been noted how the Gospels' accounts differ from their non-Christian contemporaries in offering no panorama of the coming world. But once one sees that the life which Christ offers is only offered and appropriated through taking up one's cross in obedience to the suffering and loving "son of man," and realizes that we only truly live by bearing about in our bodies the putting to death of Jesus, then a very different view of a Christian's life emerges. So far from being placed beyond the reach of death, one is daily exposed to it and daily courts it if the call of Jesus and his God demands it. No form of existence could be more thoroughly "earthed" in this world and its sufferings.

In thus linking "resurrection" and "life" with Jesus' call to his followers to gain life by losing their lives and with the apostle Paul's experience of finding life in sharing Jesus' being put to death, we find ourselves returning to the themes of the last two chapters. In the one we saw the harsh reality of the way that Jesus' first followers were called upon to tread, a way of life threatened again and again by death; in the other we saw how on the eve of his crucifixion Jesus sought to evoke amongst his closest followers a sense of solidarity and sharing in his suffering. In this way talk of "resurrection" and "life" need say nothing about our existence after death, but potentially a great deal about our existence here and now. And that is of more value, for, in my experience at least, my interest is focused, not on some existence beyond the grave, but on what lies between now and my end; I am concerned, in other words, with questions like "What can I (still) do now with the time that remains to me?" but also with the realization that my present condition might so deteriorate that death would be a welcome release, coupled with a thankfulness (and surprise) that that stage has not yet been reached.

6

Epilogue

Christian wanderers at least have some firm ground beneath their feet, though probably not as much as they would like, both in the evidence of the earliest days of the Christian movement and in their own day in the existence of the Christian church. However, that firm ground may be treacherously overlaid by legendary and speculative elements, particularly in the case of the founding events of the Christian movement and above all the person of Jesus. As for the contemporary church, its many forms are each laden with their own history and the ensuing assumptions and pretensions to which that history has given birth. Nor may Christians find that the firm ground, the reality, is always to their taste, when even the work and message of the earthly Jesus may betray things that are displeasing, outmoded, or open to criticism in various ways. Even more, it hardly needs to be said that many Christians may find the contemporary church, even their own particular branch of it, wanting in many respects.

The past reality of Jesus and the earliest church is not a matter of certainty but of probability, in some matters a very high degree of probability. Knowledge of past events

EPILOGUE

in general, and particularly events lying so far in the past, is dependent on evidence and inference, but in this case it would be a case of excessive skepticism to say that we had no knowledge at all of these origins of the Christian movement. In the preceding chapters I have attempted to sift out what can be asserted with confidence about some aspects of those beginnings, to lay bare the reality of the starting-point of this movement. That starting-point has in turn served as a point of reference for succeeding generations, to varying degrees and in various ways, and it is right that they should refer to it. Otherwise one would introduce a fundamental shift in the Christian church's self-understanding, and the whole edifice would, as it were, hang in the air, uprooted. Is this reality that it is then its own justification and can it be? In other words, is its nature such that one must judge it positively and simply applaud its intrinsic worth for humanity and the world?

That would be problematic if, as we saw, the social phenomenon of the Christian church today is in fact a very varied one, as it has been to some degree from the beginning. Would it not be grotesque to pass a blanket judgment on this institution in its entirety, either for or against it? Rather it is surely necessary to differentiate between the various manifestations of the Christian community and the life and values that we find there. Moreover, we need to do that while all the time bearing in mind that most of them at least will be claiming in their life and values to be following Jesus. Some may stop short of that and say that they seek at least to follow one of the varying traditions found in the New Testament while others may be allowed to follow others. In that they would be showing a broad-mindedness and tolerance not shared by some of the New Testament writers themselves, if one recalls, for instance, Paul's bitter struggles with Jewish Christians who sought to impose the observance of the Jewish law on his non-Jewish converts. Confronted with the broad spectrum of forms of Christianity that we find today, sometimes even within one and the same Christian denomination, we are, at any rate, forced to make choices. If the New Testament itself is varied in its witness, containing views that are hard to reconcile with one another (e.g., Paul over against the Letter of James or the Gospel of Matthew), then we may well have to make choices there too, and to do that it would be natural to invoke the help of Jesus himself and what we know of him. In both our sifting out of the reports of the origins of Christianity and in our weighing up of the pros and cons of the different manifestations of the Christian life and faith today it will still be unavoidable that a large role will be played by our subjective preferences; here we must trust to a sort of sense of direction in finding the way that has led from the beginning and leads out into the future.

Now the image of the "way" used here might seem to imply knowledge of that future, a goal, but what is that "goal" if we set aside "heaven" or an afterlife or at least regard these as possibly or probably illusory, and certainly not sufficiently well delineated or of proven existence to be much help here? If our journey takes us beyond this world, as it will, then we need to recognize that we know little about that "beyond." It is our present existence, our way through it, and our shaping of it with which we need guidance. And here we have the help of voices from the past and from the present, those of Jesus and Christians and others, past and present. None of those voices are to be followed unquestioningly, even that of Jesus, if he may have been led to follow in many respects the assumptions of his time. So each of us has to make sense for ourselves out of the messages of these competing voices, helped by the efforts of our contemporaries to achieve this same goal.

EPILOGUE

It is true that the Johannine Jesus affirms "I am the way" (John 14:6), and that at first sounds encouraging, but unfortunately it is not as simple as that for those who would follow him. For one thing, as we have already seen, this evangelist has so overlaid the this-worldly reality of the earthly Jesus with many trappings of the heavenly that it makes it difficult for mere mortals to follow him, not being aware, like him, of their past glory with God or knowing for certain that their knowledge and will is at one with God's (although some may give the impression that they do!) or that they have power over their own life and death. Without such navigation aids one's way is far less sure as to its course and destination. Even the Jesus of the Synoptic Gospels is no infallible guide: the picture of him painted by these evangelists has also been overlaid, though to a lesser extent, by the views of later Christians, including, of course, the evangelists themselves. And we have seen too that, in fact, Jesus himself may well have taken over many views held by his contemporaries, including ones that we today would not wish to endorse or follow. Nevertheless, there is enough there that both probably stems from Jesus' teaching and offers us even today pointers to a way to follow through our very different world, very different, but still beset with similar problems of human imperfection and inadequacy, still needing help in living with our world and our fellow human beings. It is to be noted, however, that this guidance is derived from Jesus, without being dependent on an appeal to some other-worldly or supernatural reality. This would be an advantage in the light of the uncertainty that surrounds the question of the nature and existence of such a reality. It is true that both Jesus and his followers—then and today—believed that their way was also sanctioned and undergirded by some such reality that they called God, but if the basis of that belief has by now worn thin and its content is shrouded in mystery, then it is more satisfactory to set that factor aside. We are then left with the this-worldly voices that may guide us on our way.

For Further Reading

I have dealt in some earlier works and in more detail with a number of the themes and questions touched on here, in particular:

Beyond Resurrection. London: SCM, 1999.
A History of the First Christians. London: T. & T. Clark, 2004.
Jesus and the Historians. WUNT 269. Tübingen: Mohr Siebeck, 2010.
The Death of Jesus: Some Reflections on Jesus-Traditions and Paul. WUNT 299; Tübingen: Mohr Siebeck, 2013.
The God of Jesus—Our God? Eugene, OR: Cascade, 2014.

www.ingramcontent.com/pod-product-compliance
Lightning Source LLC
Chambersburg PA
CBHW022119090426
42743CB00008B/920